Patrick Henry: Patriot, Orator and Anti-Federalist:

Non-Fiction Common Core Readings

Table of Contents

From: **HOMES OF AMERICAN STATESMEN**
Illustrated with engravings on wood, from drawings by Doplerand Dauerreotypes: and Fac-similes of Autograph Letters
Hartford: Published by O.D. Case & CO
London; Sampson Low, Son & Company

[153]

Residence of Patrick Henry, Va.

PATRICK HENRY.

There is no "Home of an American Statesman" that may more fitly claim the leading place in this our repository than the dwelling of Patrick Henry—the earliest, the most eloquent, and the wisest of those whose high counsels first swayed us as one people and drew us to a common cause; as resolutely as ably directed that cause to its noble event; and, in a word, performing in the civil struggle all that Washington executed in the military, achieved for us existence as a nation.

In the Heroic Age, however, such as was to us the Revolution,

[154]

men build not monuments nor engrave commemorative inscriptions: those of nature, identified by rude but reverential tradition, alone attest where the founders of a race, the great-fathers of an empire, have sprung.

If there be, among the many men of that brave day, one prompter and more unfaltering than all the rest; if, among all who moved by stirring words and decisive acts the general mind of the country, there was one who more directly than any, or than all, set it in a flame not to be extinguished; if amidst those lights there was one, the day star, till whose coming there was no dawn, it was certainly Henry. It is true that, before him, Massachusetts had her quarrel with England, but not with the common sympathy of the colonies. For, averse, from her very foundation, to not merely the dominion, but the very institutions of the mother country, she had kept up with it a continual bickering, religious as well as civil; a strife at best local, often ill-tempered and factious; so that her too frequent broils, commanding little regard, would have continued to come to nothing had not an opposition to English measures sprung up in a more loyal quarter. The southern colonies, meanwhile, had always loved the parent land, both church and state, and naturally had been indulgently dealt with by its legislation. Thus, until that ill-advised measure, the Stamp Act, came, to affect all the American plantations alike, there had been nothing to draw us together in a common cause, a common resistance. The Stamp Act gave that cause, and Henry led that resistance. Young, obscure, unconnected, unaided, uncounselled, and even uncountenanced, he yet, by the sudden splendor of his eloquence, his abilities, and his dauntless resolution, carried every thing

[155]

before him; animated the whole land to a determined assertion of their rights; established for himself a boundless influence over the popular mind; used it, whenever the occasion came, to sound the signal of an unshrinking opposition to every encroachment; led the way, independently of all movements elsewhere; devised and brought about every main measure of preparation; rejected all compromise; clearly the first to see the certain issue of the contest in European interposition and the establishment of our Independence, pursued steadily that aim before even he could openly avow it: and finally, when things were ripe; assumed it for his State, instructed her deputation to propose it to all the rest, and indeed, involved them in it beyond avoidance, by setting up a regular and permanent Republican Constitution in Virginia; a step that allowed no retreat, and was not less decisive than the heroical act of Cortez, when, marching upon Mexico from his landing-place, he burnt his vessels behind him. Henry was, in a word, the Moses who led us forth from the house of bondage. If there had been an opposition before his, it was not the appointed, and would have been an ineffectual one. There had, no doubt, been Jews enough that murmured, even before he who was to deliver them appeared. We may, therefore, fitly apply to Henry, in regard to the bringing about of our Independence, all that Dryden so finely said of Bacon in science:

"Bacon, like Moses, led us forth, at last: The barren wilderness he passed; Did on the very border stand Of the blest promised land; And from the mountain-top of his exalted wit, Saw it himself and showed us it."

[156]

And yet Henry, like nearly all his illustrious fellow-laborers of freedom, sleeps in an undistinguished grave. At his death, party spirit denied to his memory the tokens of public admiration and regret, offered in that very legislature of which he had been the great light, and which, indeed, he had called into being. Since that sorry failure—for all faction should have been hushed over the body of a citizen and a man so admirable—no further notice has been taken of him; and he who merited a national monument, only less proud than that due to Washington himself, slumbers beneath an humble private one at Red Hill, the secluded residence where he died.

But we turn to those personal particulars of this extraordinary man which are appropriate to the design of the present volume. Not a few of them will be found to involve important corrections of the received account of his early years, and a new view, therefore, of his genius and character.

In that received account, his sole original biographer, Mr. Wirt—writing without any personal knowledge of him, and neglecting to consult the most obvious and authentic source of information, his four surviving sisters, ladies of condition and of remarkable intelligence—has fallen into the vulgar error, to which the peculiar position and fortunes of Mr. Henry at first gave rise, and which he afterwards, for warrantable political purposes, encouraged. When he suddenly burst out from complete obscurity, an unrivalled orator, a consummate politician, and snatched the control of legislation and of the public mind from the veteran, the college-bred, the wealthy and high-born leaders who had till then held it, the homeliness of dress which befitted his narrow circumstances, the humility of

[157]

aspect and the simplicity of manners, which were unaffected traits of his disposition, naturally assigned him in the eyes of both those who were of it and of those who looked down upon it, to the plebeian class. It suited the envy of these, it delighted the admiration of those, to regard him— that unintelligible marvel of abilities, which had thus all at once effaced every thing else—as a mere child of the people. The really skilful, who understand intellectual prodigies and never refer them to ignorance or chance, must have seen at once, through the cloud in which he stood, a great and an enlightened understanding, too competent to a high and a complex public question, not to be strong in knowledge as well as faculties. The few cannot have mistaken him for that fabulous thing, an ignorant genius; for they must have seen in his commanding and complete eloquence the art, in his masterly measures the information, of one thoroughly trained, though in secret, to the business of swaying men's minds, and of conducting their counsels, though hitherto apart from them. All but this highest class, however, of the rivals whom he at once threw into eclipse naturally sought to depreciate him as a mere declaimer, a tribunitian orator, voluble and vehement as he was rude, rash, and illiterate. Could the tapers that, at Belshazzar's feast, went out before the blaze of that marvellous handwriting on the wall, have been afterwards permitted to give their opinion of it, they would, of course, have talked disdainfully of its beam, as mere phosphorus or some other low pyrotechnic trick. Such was the reputation which the vanquished magnates in general, and their followers, endeavored to fix upon the young subverter of their ascendency. He was not of one of the old aristocratic families; he was a low person, therefore he had never been

[158]

within the walls of a college, still less had he, like many of them, finished, with the graces of foreign travel, a public discipline of learning; he was, therefore, by their report, illiterate, although, certainly, in his performances, all the best effects of education were manifest, without its parade. While they called him ignorant, he always proved himself to know whatever the occasion demanded, and able victoriously to instruct foe and friend. Shunning, from his sense, all assumption, and from his modesty, all display, he never pulled out the purse of his acquirements to chink it merely, but only to pay; so that no man could tell what he had left in the bottom of his pocket; and thus, a ragged-looking Fortunatus, he always surprised men with his unguessed resources. Strange powers, undoubtedly, he had, that must have not a little confounded the judgment of the best observers; unexercised in the forum, he had risen up a consummate master of the whole art of moving in discourse the understanding or the passions; unpractised in public affairs, he had only to appear in them, in order to stand the first politician of his day; unversed in the business and the strategy of deliberative assemblies, he had only to become a member of one, in order to be its adroitest parliamentary tactician. As he was dexterous without practice, so was he prudent without experience; for, from the first he shone out as the wisest man in all the public councils. He seems to have escaped all that tribute of error which youth must almost invariably pay, as the price of eminence in public affairs; he fell into no theory, he indulged no vision, he never once committed a blunder; in short, ripe from the beginning, he appeared to be by instinct and the mere gift of nature, whatever others slowly become only by the aid of art and experience.

[159]

Bred up in seclusion, though (as the high cultivation of his sisters testified to all who knew them) in a household whose very atmosphere was knowledge, he had, beyond a good acquaintance with Latin, the rudiments of Greek, French, mathematics, and an early familiarity with the best English authors—those of the Elizabethan age, of the Commonwealth, and of Queen Anne's day—received little direct instruction; none, but from his father and books, his early companions, so that his scholastic instruction was really slender. But he had been taught, betimes, to love knowledge and how to work it out for himself; how, in a word, to accomplish what best unfolds a great genius, self-education. For schools and colleges—admirable contrivances as they are for keeping up among mankind a common method and a common stock of information—are but suited, as they were but designed, for the common run of men. Applying to all the same mechanical process; bringing to the same level the genius and the dunce, they act excellently to repair the original inequality, sometimes so vast, with which nature deals out understanding among the human race. In a word, they are capital machines for bringing about an average of talent; but it is at the expense of those bright parts which occasionally come, that they do it. Their methods clap in the same couples him who can but creep and him who would soar; harness in the same cart the plough-horse and the courser. The highest genius must be its own sole method-maker, its own entire rule. From what it has done, rules are deduced; but for its inferiors, not for it: its whole existence is exceptional, original; and whatever, in its disciplining, would tend to make it otherwise, serves but to check and to diminish its development.

[160]

No greater error, therefore, than to suppose that a man as extraordinary as Patrick Henry, who, mature from the first, rose up a consummate speaker and reasoner, and, amongst men of large abilities, knowledge, and experience, constantly showed himself, in matters the weightiest and the most difficult, superior to them all, could have been uneducated. In reality he had learned of the best possible master, for such a man—himself. That he knew, that he even knew more solidly, because more effectually and to the purpose, than all those around him, the great subjects with which he dealt so wonderfully, is beyond all question. Now, though the genius of Mr. Henry was prodigious, and though there be things which genius does, as it were, intuitively and spontaneously, there are other things which are not knowable, even by genius itself, without study; which the utmost genius cannot extemporize, cannot produce from nothing, cannot make without their materials previously amassed in its mind, cannot understand without their necessary particulars accumulated in advance; and it was in just such things—the highest civil ability, which comes of wisdom, not genius; the greatest eloquence which cannot be formed but by infinite art and labor—that he stood up at all times supreme. The sagacity of statesmanship with which he looked through the untried affairs of this country, saw through systems and foretold consequences, has never been surpassed; and his eloquence, judged (as we have alone the means of judging it) by its effects, has never been equalled.

Such then, even upon the traditionary facts out of which his biographer has shaped into a mere fable his sudden rise and his anomalous abilities, is, of necessity, the rational theory

[161]

of Mr. Henry's greatness. But, without any resort to induction, the simple truth, if Mr. Wirt had sought it in the natural quarter, would have conducted him to the same conclusions as we have just set forth.

At the time when Mr. Wirt collected his materials, he was yet, though of fine natural abilities, by no means the solid man that he by and by became. His fancy was exuberant, his taste florid, his judgment unformed. Himself in high repute for a youthful and gaudy eloquence, which, however, he afterwards exchanged for a style of great severity and vigor—he had been urged to his immature and ambitious undertaking, by admirers who conceived him to be little less than a second Henry. His besetting idea seems to be much akin to Dr. Johnson's "who drives fat oxen should himself be fat:" namely that the life of a great orator should be written by a great orator; and that he was to show not only Mr. Henry but himself eloquent. In general his book does him credit, as merely a literary performance, although sadly deformed, in what were intended for its best passages, by an inflation of which he must have been afterwards greatly ashamed, as a sin against all style, but especially that proper to his subject—the historic. Let us add—in simple justice to a man of great virtues and elevation, as well as gentleness of mind and feelings, whose memory has upon us, besides, the claim of public respect and of hereditary friendship—that his biography, wherever his own, is, in spite of party spirit, written with the most honorable candor, and vindicates Mr. Henry with equal fairness and ability from the aspersions cast upon his conduct in the "Alien and Sedition" business by the Jeffersonian faction. Wherever he (Mr. Wirt) has depended upon his own researches alone, he displays

[162]

both diligence and discrimination; but unhappily, he accepted the loose popular traditions, which are never any thing but a tissue of old women's tales; he relied upon a mass of casual contributions, chiefly derived from the same legendary sources or from uncertain, confused, and (as himself lets us see) often contradictory memories; and above all, he adopted implicitly the information supplied by a certain Thomas Jefferson; who, besides being a person of whom the sagacious and upright Henry cherished a very ill opinion—so that *he* could not well be supposed a very special repository of the orator's personal confidences—was a gentleman who had all his life driven rather the largest and most lucrative trade in the calumny of nearly all the best and greatest of his contemporaries, that has ever been carried on in these United States, much as that sort of commerce has long flourished and yet flourishes amongst us. Upon such things he had come to a splendid political fortune while he lived, and when he died, with a pious solicitude to provide for his posterity, he bequeathed to his grandson all the unspent capital stock of his slanders (his Memoirs and Ana) to carry on the old business with and keep up the greatness of the family.

The effect of all this was to turn what before was strange or obscure, in Henry's history, into little better than a fable, a sort of popular and poetic myth of eloquence, in which the great speaker and statesman fades away into a fiction, a mere creation of the fancy, scarcely more real or probable than the account in old Master Tooke's "Pantheon," of Orpheus's drawing the rocks and trees and the very wild beasts along with him by his powers of song. Nay, in one main point, Master Tooke's legend more consults verisimilitude: for *he*, instead of

[163]

shocking all probability by representing his hero to have been without education, sends him as private pupil to the Muses themselves, who are reputed to have kept, then as now, the best Greek and Latin colleges a-going.

It is certainly true, in excuse for all this, that the mighty men who, for their exploits and services, became the demigods of fable, "the fair humanities of old religion," had scarcely more struck the excited imagination of their times than had Henry. Like theirs was the obscurity of his birth, the mystery of his education, the marvel of his achievements. Of his many great speeches, scarcely one uncorrupted passage can be said to survive; so that even of that which all felt and know we have but the faintest shadow. A fragmentary thought is all of genuine that is left us out of a whole immortal harangue; some powerful ejaculation stands for an entire oration, and dimly suggests, not explains its astonishing effects. To all purpose historic of his eloquence, he might just as well have lived before alphabetic writing was invented. At best, the oratory that entrances, agitates, enraptures, transports every man in a whole assembly, and hurries him totally away, thrilling and frenzied with sensations as vehement as novel, sets all reporting, all stenography at defiance. Before it, shorthand—at most, the dim reflection of such things; a cold copy, a poor parody where it is not a burlesque of speech in its great bursts—drops its pen, and forgets even to translate; which, after all (*haud inexpertus loquor*), is the utmost it can do. But of not even such translation did Mr. Henry, upon any occasion but two,[11] receive the advantage such as it is. Every

[164]

where in these the single but skilful reporter confesses, by many a summary in parenthesis, that at certain passages he lost himself in the speaker, and could not even attempt to render him. Thus it comes that, of his transcendent harangues—those which made or directed the Revolution—we have only a few scattered sentences, and the seemingly amazed descriptions which attest their extraordinary effects. There is but one exception: a version, to appearance tolerably entire, though still evidently but a sketch, of his "Liberty or Death" speech, when, on the 20th March, 1775, he told the Convention of Virginia, assembled in the "Old Church" at Richmond (St. Johns), that "they must fight," and moved to arm and organize the militia. This, even in its existing form, is a prodigiously noble speech, full of vigor in the argument, full of passion in the appeals, breathing every where the utmost fire of the warrior, orator, patriot, and sage. Fitly uttered, it is still—though of course it must have lost greatly in the transmission—a discourse to rouse a whole nation invincibly to arms, if their cause and their courage were worthy of it. That speech evidently, and that speech alone, is, in the main, the true thunder of Henry: all the others are but the mustard-bowl.

Old Church Richmond, Va.

But though from all these causes, he already, in Mr. Wirt's day, stood, as seen through the fast-gathered haze of tradition, a huge but shadowy figure, it was the business of the biographer, instead of merely showing him to us in that popular light, to set him in a true one. The critical historian clears up such mists, defines such shadows, and calls them back not only to substance but proportion, color, life, the very pressure and body of the times. What if the historic truth had passed

[165]

into a poetic fable? Mr. Wirt should have dealt with it, not as a bard, a rhapsodist, but a philosophical mythologist, who from fable itself sifts out the unwritten facts of a day, when fable was the only form of history.

Besides, however, adopting for the fundamental facts of Mr. Henry's character all these false sources, his biographer utterly neglected (as we have already intimated) the most obvious and the most natural ones. He had then four surviving sisters, women not merely of condition but intellectually remarkable.

To none of these did Mr. Wirt resort for any domestic particulars of his early life, which of course none knew so well as they. Well acquainted with them all—sprung from one of them—we have cause to know the astonishment with which they met this written account of his early years and his breeding up. Had Mr. Wirt personally known these highly cultivated and very superior ladies, distinguished as they were for the completeness and solidity of their old-fashioned education, he must have seen at once that his own story of Henry's youthful institution and ways is about as true as it is that Achilles was born of a sea-goddess, had a centaur for his private tutor, and was fed upon lion's marrow to make him valiant.

His very lineage was literary. His father, John Henry, a Scottish gentleman of Aberdeen, was a man of good birth, of learned education, and, when he migrated to Virginia, of easy fortune. He was the nephew of Robertson, the great historian of his own country and of ours. The name of his mother, Jane Robertson, an admirable and accomplished person, is still preserved and transmitted among her female descendants. His cousin, David Henry, was the associate editor of the "Gentleman's Magazine," then a leading publication, with

[166]

Edward Cave, the last of the learned printers; whose brother-in-law and successor he became. The family bred many of its members for the church, which in Britain implies such influence as secures preferment. John's younger brother, Patrick, thus taking orders, received a rectorship near him, and followed him to this country. In those days of Episcopacy, benefices drew after them not merely comfortable reverence, but goodly emolument and even authority in civil life; so that the parsons were a power in the State. All this Patrick, a man worthy of it, employed. His brother already possessed it; and thus both took their station among the gentry, though not the aristocracy, of the land—its untitled nobility: for, in effect, such an order, sustained by primogeniture and entails, then existed throughout lower or tide-water Virginia.

John attained to the command of the regiment of his county, to its surveyorship, and to the presiding chair of its magistracy; stations then never conferred but upon leading men in the community. More careless, however, of his private interests than of the public, without exactly wasting his fortune, he gradually frittered it away; and though he repaired it for a time, by an advantageous marriage with the young and wealthy widow (a Winston by birth) of his most intimate friend, Col. John Syme, of the Rocky Mills, yet before the tenth year of Patrick, his second son (born 29th May, 1736), he found himself so straitened as to have need to make himself an income by setting up in his house a private classical school. Assisted to this by the reputation of being one of the best scholars in the country, he taught for a number of years with great approval the children of his friends and his own; abandoning the pursuit only when one of its inducements—the

[167]

education of his own sons and daughters (two of the former and five of the latter)—had ceased.

Under such circumstances, and especially when we repeat that those four of his daughters whom we knew were persons greatly admired for the masculine goodness and extent of their education, it may be judged how likely, how possible it is that Patrick, with his boundless aptitude—always, in after life, applied most rapidly and successfully to whatever he had need to understand—can have grown up to manhood almost uninstructed, ignorant, and idle. Genius, of which it is the very essence that it has an uncontrollable affinity for the knowledge proper to its caste, has often been seen to surmount obstacles seemingly invincible to its information; never yet wilfully, incorrigibly, and in spite of every influence around, to shut out the open and easy daylight of intelligence, and darken itself into voluntary duncedom. The thing, we repeat is a flat, a bald and a flagrant impossibility. You might as well tell us that a young eagle, instead of taking to the sky as soon as its pinions were grown, has, though neither caged nor clipped, remained contented on foot and preferred to run about the barn-yard with the dunghill fowls. No! your "mute Miltons" and your harmless Cromwells sound very prettily to the fancy, but in plain fact, were no Miltons unless they sang, no Cromwells unless they conquered. Genius and Heroism—the most strenuous of human things—were never dull, slothful, idle; never slighted opportunity, but always make, if they do not find it.

Accordingly, the sisters of Mr. Henry always asserted that, whatever their brother might appear abroad, he was a close voluntary student at home; exploring not only his father's

[168]

library, which was large and good, but whatever other books he could lay his hands upon; dwelling, with an especial delight, upon certain great authors, of whom he seemed to make his masters; but cultivating assiduously what was then called "polite learning," and merited the name, along with history at large, and that of the free states of antiquity, and of England in particular. His great favorites were Livy and Virgil; not (as Mr. Wirt supposes of the former) in a translation, but the original. That the sisters were right on this point is sufficiently proved by the fact that, a few years ago, his Latin Virgil was in existence, its margins all filled with his manuscript notes. We need hardly say that he who was not content with Dryden as a translator was clearly not a-going to take up with poor old Philemon Holland, then the current English disfigurer of the most animated and picturesque of historians. Henry's sisters indeed, and the only one of his schoolfellows that we have ever met, were persuaded that he read Latin almost as readily as English. Mr. Wirt himself had learned that the great Paduan was ever in his boyish hands; now, that single point established, he might without hesitation have proceeded to five clear and important inferences: first, that no boy has a favorite book but because he is fond of books generally; secondly, that when his favorite is, though of the highest merit, a very unusual one, he must not only have read much, but with great discrimination: thirdly, that if his favorite was in a special class (not a mere miscellanist) he was well read in that class, addicted to it: fourthly, that he was enamored of such a favorite for his matchless merits, both of matter and of style; his sensibility to the former of which particulars implied information, to the latter a

[169]

well-formed taste: fifthly, that no mere translation of Livy—especially not flat, tame old Holland—nothing short of the golden original, could have inspired such a Livian affection. But this is not all; when—coming to be put into the possession of the scanty remaining body of Mr. Henry's papers (ill-preserved by his not very wise progeny) and invited to write his life more authentically—we ourselves began first to study his speeches and his mind critically, it did not take us long to perceive, what is indeed easily seen, that Mr. Henry's early passion for Livy—born of course of Livy's conformity to his genius—had deeply tinged the peculiar style of his eloquence, the peculiar character of his politics, was, in sooth, the immediate source of both; that the harangues in Livy had been his models of discourse; that the sentiments of public magnanimity, which Livy every where, and we may say Livy alone breathes, were transfused into Henry's spirit, and gave to his ideas of a state that singular grandeur, that loftiness, that heroism, which fills and informs them. His love of freedom even—his republicanism—was such as Livy's; popular, yet patrician: not your levelled liberty, too low to last, which, to keep down the naturally great, sets up the base on high; but a freedom consistent with the eminence and the subordination of natural orders mutually dependent; equal under the law, but distinct in their power to serve the state, as bringing to its aid, this rank higher counsels and obligations, that, force and numbers; in short, not merely a tumultuary, a mob liberty, but a social and a regulated concert of all classes, the absolute predominance of none; a republican, not a democratic aim. Less learned than Milton, certainly, but of a highly kindred spirit, he was very like him in his general political system; but was

[170]

more practical, better acquainted with men. The one had more of the poetical element in him, the other more of the political. Both were deeply religious; without which no man can be a safe politician. Each towered above all the men of his day, except one, a warrior; and nearly such relation as Milton held to Cromwell did Henry hold to Washington. Alike in the antique cast of their minds, they were yet alike in being, withal, thoroughly English in their notion of actual freedom: for Henry's mind was just as little touched with any of the Jeffersonian fancies of Frenchified liberty as Milton's own. Both were of the historic, not the so-called philosophic school of politics: for history was evidently the only treatise on government that either thought worthy of any attention. If they had ever stooped to the systematic writers, from the great sources (wise histories) out of which those writers can at most draw, it can only have been to despise nearly every mother's son of them. Finally, alike in so many things, they were not unlike in their fate: both "fell upon evil times," and lost their public credit in the land of which they had matchlessly vindicated the public cause: Milton died sightless, and Henry too blind for the light of the Virginia abstractions.

Every thing confutes the vulgar theory of his greatness. Had he been ignorant at his first rise, the growth of his talent, as well as of his knowledge, would have been traceable in his performances; but on the contrary, he burst out, from the first, mature and finished. By the universal consent, his very earliest speeches were quite equal to any thing he ever after pronounced. Had these been at sixteen, it would go far to prove that his eloquence, his ability, and even his information came (as such things never came in any other instance) without cultivation: but his first speech, that in "the parson's

[171]

cause," at Hanover Court House, in 1763, when he was twenty-nine years old; the same period of life at which Demosthenes and Cicero shone out; a period after which there may be large additions to artificial knowledge, but can seldom be any to the natural splendor of the faculties.

We have known many who knew Mr. Henry, in the entire unreserve of that domestic life, in which he so much loved to unbend himself. All such agreed that he was a man of very great and very various information. He read every thing. At home, his interval between an early dinner and supper-time (after which he gave himself up to conversation with his friends, or to sport with his children, or to music on the violin and flute, which he played) was always consecrated to study: he withdrew from company to his office and books. His very manner of reading was such as few attain, and marks the great and skilful dealer with other men's thoughts: he seldom read a book regularly on; but seemed only to glance his eye down the pages, and, as it were, to gallop athwart the volume; and yet, when he had thus strid through it, knew better than any body else all that was worth knowing in it contents. A learned physician who dwelt near him, told us, in speaking of this wide range of his knowledge, that he had, for instance, to his surprise, found him to be a good chemist, at a time when an acquaintance with that science was almost confined to medical men. Except in private, however, he kept the secret of his own attainments, content to let them appear only in their effects. This was, originally, out of his singular modesty; but by and by when his vanquished rivals of college-breeding sought to depreciate him as low-born and uneducated, he from policy conformed to imputations which heightened the wonder of his performances and therefore added to his success.

[172]

Let us add one more fact, substantive and significant. The range of a man's mind, the very particulars of his studies may usually, when he is not a mere book-collector or other affector of letters, be pretty definitely ascertained from the contents of his library. In that view, finding that a list of Mr. Henry's was embraced in the records of the Court of Probate of his county, we examined and copied it. For that day, his library, besides its merely professional contents, is quite a large one—some five hundred volumes, mostly good and solid. We found it to contain the usual series of Greek school-books, probably all he had ever read; for the language was then slightly learnt in Virginia: a good many of the Latin authors, and various French ones. The last language we know, from other sources, that he understood. Now, he was the man in the world the least likely to have got or to keep books that he did not comprehend.

Such was the enigma of Patrick Henry's mind; and such is its clear solution: a solution which, at least, must be confessed to substitute the rational for the irrational, the possible for the impossible, the positive of domestic evidence for the negative of popular tradition.

Apart, however, from such testimony, there were other proofs that should have suggested themselves to the anatomist of life character, the physiologist of his genius. When we ourselves first began minutely to consider his speeches, their effects, all that is told of the manner in which those effects were brought about, the reach and the diversity of his powers, their admirable adaptation to all occasions and to all audiences—for he swayed all men alike by his eloquence, the low and the high, the ignorant and the learned; the unapproached

[173]

dramatic perfection of his voice, gesture, manner, and whole delivery; his mastery, not only in speech, but off the tribune and man to man, of all that can affect either men's reason or their imagination, we could not, for our lives, help coming to the conclusion that all this must be skill, not chance; and that instead of being the mere child of nature, he was the most consummate artist that ever lived. Nature bestows marvellous things, but these are not within even her gift. She gives the gold, but she does not work it into every beautiful form; she gives the diamond, but she does not cut it; she bestows the marble, but did not carve the Olympian Jove nor the Belvidere Apollo. In fine, we had, in much acquaintance with men the ornaments of the public life of our times, been accustomed to understand all the minute mechanism of civil abilities; and when we came to examine closely this matchless piece of machinery, we could not avoid believing, in spite of all assertions to the contrary, that each particular part, however nice and small, must have been made by hand and most painfully put together. And thus, perceiving every thing else in this prodigious speaker to have been so masterly, we became convinced that his style, his diction must have been, in the main, as excellent as every thing else about him. It could not have been otherwise. He whose thought was so high and pure, whose fancy was so rich, and the mere outward auxiliaries of whose discourse (voice, and action) had been so laboriously perfected, can, by no possibility, have failed to make himself equally the master of expression. What we have as his, is mere reporter's English; and no man is to be judged by that slop of sentences into which he is put and melted away by their process. In that menstruum of words, all substances are alike. It is the true universal solvent, so long sought, that

[174]

acts upon every thing and turns it into liquid babble. Mr Henry knew and often practised, not only upon the multitude but the refined; the power of a homely dialect, and saw how wise or brave or moving things may be made to come with a strangely redoubled effect, in the extremest plainness of rustic speech. His occasional resort to this, however, of course struck much upon the common attention and got him the reputation, among other foolish reputations, of habitually using such locutions; when, in reality, he was master of all modes of discourse alike, and only employed always that which best suited his purpose.

There is yet one more false notion, in regard to him, which Mr. Wirt has done much to propagate: the notion, we mean, that Henry never condescended to be less than the great orator; that, instead of sometimes going about his business on foot, like other lawyers and legislators, he rode for ever in a sort of triumphal car of eloquence, dragging along a captive crowd at his conquering wheels; and, in short, that

"He could not ope His mouth, but out there flew a trope."

On the contrary, no man was ever less the oration-maker. He never used his eloquence but as he used every thing else—just when it was wanted. In the mass of public business, eloquence is out of place, and could not be attended to. A man who was always eloquent would soon lose all authority in a public body. Mr. Henry kept up always the very greatest, and merited it, by taking a leading part in all important matters and making more and better business speeches than any body else.

A long preliminary this; but we trust not uninteresting.

[175]

It was, at any event, necessary that we should first, in the Bentonian phrase, "vindicate the truth of history," and set a great character in its proper public light, before passing to those humble particulars of private life to which we now proceed.

In person, he was tall and rather spare, but of limbs round enough for either vigor or grace. He had, however, a slight stoop, such as very thoughtful people are apt to contract. In public, his aspect was remarkable for quiet gravity. It seems to have been a rule with him never to laugh and hardly to smile, before the vulgar. In their presence he wore an air always fit to excite at once their sympathy and their reverence; modest, even to humility; and yet most imposing. In all this he played no assumed, though he could not have played a more skilful part: for the occasion and the presence appear always to have so duly and so strongly affected him, as at once to transform him into what was, at each instant, fittest. Thus his art, of which we have already spoken, might well be consummate; for he was all that, for mere purposes of effect, he should have seemed to be, the very impersonation of the cause and the feelings proper to the hour. Great wisdom, indeed, an unshrinking courage, and yet an equal prudence, a patriotism the most fervent, a profound sensibility, a rare love of justice, yet a spirit of the greatest gentleness and humanity, and in a word, the highest virtues, public and private, crowned with a disinterestedness, an absence of all ambition most singular in a democracy (which above all things breeds the contrary) made him—if Cicero be right—the greatest of orators, because the most virtuous of men that ever possessed that natural gift. No man ever knew men better, singly or in the mass; none ever better knew how to sway them; but none ever less abused that power, for he seems ever to have felt, in

[176]

a religious force, the solemnity of all those public functions, which so few now regard. It was probably the weight of this feeling, along with his singular modesty, that made him shun official honors as earnestly as others seek them. It is evident that no power, nor dignity, nor even fame could dazzle him. It was only at the public command that he accepted trusts from his State; and he always laid them down as soon as duty permitted. All offers of Federal dignities,[12] up to the highest, he rejected. He had served his State only in perilous times, when (as the Devil says in Milton) to be highest was only to be exposed foremost to the bolts of the dreaded enemy; or at some conjuncture of civil danger; but when peace and ease had come and ambition was the only lure to office, he would not have it.

If, however, he was thus grave, on what he considered the solemn stage of public life, he made himself ample amends in all that can give cheerfulness to the calm of retirement in the country. When at last permitted to attend to his private fortune, he speedily secured an ample one. It was enjoyed, whenever business allowed him to be at home, in a profuse and general, but solid and old-fashioned hospitality, of which the stout and semi-baronial supplies were abundantly drawn from his own large and well-managed domain. His house was usually filled with friends, its dependencies with their retinue

[177]

and horses. But crowds, besides, came and went; all were received and entertained with cordiality. The country all about thronged to see the beloved and venerated man, as soon as it went abroad that he was come back. Some came merely to see him; the rest to get his advice on law and all other matters. To the poor, it was gratuitous; to even the rich without a fee, except where he thought the case made it necessary to go to law. All took his counsel as if it had been an oracle's, for nobody thought there was any measure to "Old Patrick's" sense, integrity, or good nature. This concourse began rather betimes, for those who lived near often came to breakfast, where all were welcomed and made full. The larder seemed never to get lean. Breakfast over, creature-comforts, such as might console the belated for its loss, were presently set forth on side-tables in the wide entrance hall. Of these—the solid, not the liquid parts of a rural morning's meal—breakfast without its slops, and such as, if need were, might well stand for a dinner, all further comers helped themselves as the day or their appetites advanced. Meanwhile, the master saw and welcomed all with the kindliest attention, asked of their household, listened to their affairs, gave them his view, contented all. These audiences seldom ceased before noon or the early dinner. To this a remaining party of from twenty to thirty often sat down. It was always, according to the wont of such houses in that well-fed land, a meal beneath which the tables groaned, and whose massive old Saxon dishes would have made a Frenchman sweat. Every thing is excellent at these lavish feasts; but they have no luxuries save such as are home-grown. They are, however, for all that is substantial and plain, the very summit of good cheer. At Governor Henry's, they never failed to be, besides,

[178]

seasoned with his conversation, which at table always grew gay and even gamesome. The dinner ended, he betook himself, as already told, to his studies until supper, after which he again gave himself up to enjoyment. In this manner came, with the kindliest and most cheerful approach, the close of his days; upon which there rested not a stain nor (such had been through life his personal benignity) a hostility. Except tyrants and other public enemies, he had lived at peace with man and God, achieving most surprising and illustrious things, and content, save the sight of his liberated country, with little reward beyond that which he bore in his own approving bosom.

Give Me Liberty or Give Me Death Speech

t. John's Church, Richmond, VirginiaMarch 23, 1775.

MR. PRESIDENT: No man thinks more highly than I do of the patriotism, as well as abilities, of the very worthy gentlemen who have just addressed the House. But different men often see the same subject in different lights; and, therefore, I hope it will not be thought disrespectful to those gentlemen if, entertaining as I do, opinions of a character very opposite to theirs, I shall speak forth my sentiments freely, and without reserve. This is no time for ceremony. The question before the House is one of awful moment to this country. For my own part, I consider it as nothing less than a question of freedom or slavery; and in proportion to the magnitude of the subject ought to be the freedom of the debate. It is only in this way that we can hope to arrive at truth, and fulfil the great responsibility which we hold to God and our country. Should I keep back my opinions at such a time, through fear of giving offence, I should consider myself as guilty of treason towards my country, and of an act of disloyalty toward the majesty of heaven, which I revere above all earthly kings.

Mr. President, it is natural to man to indulge in the illusions of hope. We are apt to shut our eyes against a painful truth, and listen to the song of that siren till she transforms us into beasts. Is this the part of wise men, engaged in a great and arduous struggle for liberty? Are we disposed to be of the number of those who, having eyes, see not, and, having ears, hear not, the things which so nearly concern their temporal salvation? For my part, whatever anguish of spirit it may cost, I am willing to know the whole truth; to know the worst, and to provide for it.

I have but one lamp by which my feet are guided; and that is the lamp of experience. I know of no way of judging of the future but by the past. And judging by the past, I wish to know what there has been in the conduct of the British ministry for the last ten years, to justify those hopes with which gentlemen have been pleased to solace themselves, and the House? Is it that insidious smile with which our petition has been lately received? Trust it not, sir; it will prove a snare to your feet. Suffer not yourselves to be betrayed with a kiss. Ask yourselves how this gracious reception of our petition comports with these war-like preparations which cover our waters and darken our land. Are fleets and armies necessary to a work of love and reconciliation? Have we shown ourselves so unwilling to be reconciled, that force must be called in to win back our love? Let us not deceive ourselves, sir. These are the implements of war and subjugation; the last arguments to which kings resort. I ask, gentlemen, sir, what means this martial array, if its purpose be not to force us to submission? Can gentlemen assign any other possible motive for it? Has Great Britain any enemy, in this quarter of the world, to call for all this accumulation of navies and armies? No, sir, she has none. They are meant for us; they can be meant for no other. They are sent over to bind and rivet upon us those chains which the British ministry have been so long forging. And what have we to oppose to them? Shall we try argument? Sir, we have been trying that for the last ten years. Have we anything new to offer upon the subject? Nothing. We have held the subject up in every light of which it is capable; but it has been all in vain. Shall we resort to entreaty and humble supplication? What terms shall we find which have not been already exhausted? Let us not, I beseech you, sir, deceive ourselves. Sir, we have done everything that could be done, to avert the storm which is now coming on. We have petitioned; we have remonstrated; we have supplicated; we have prostrated ourselves before the throne, and have implored its interposition to arrest the tyrannical hands of the ministry and Parliament. Our petitions have been slighted; our remonstrances have produced additional violence and insult; our supplications have been disregarded; and we have been spurned, with contempt, from the foot of the throne. In vain, after these things, may we indulge the fond hope of peace and reconciliation. There is no longer any room for hope. If we wish to be free² if we mean to preserve inviolate those inestimable privileges for which we have been so long contending²if we mean not basely to abandon the noble struggle in which we have been so long engaged, and which we have pledged ourselves never to abandon until the glorious object of our contest shall be obtained, we must fight! I repeat it, sir, we must fight! An appeal to arms and to the God of Hosts is all that is left us!

They tell us, sir, that we are weak; unable to cope with so formidable an adversary. But when shall we be stronger? Will it be the next week, or the next year? Will it be when we are totally disarmed, and when a British guard shall be stationed in every house? Shall we gather strength by irresolution and inaction? Shall we acquire the means of effectual resistance, by lying supinely on our backs, and hugging the delusive phantom of hope, until our enemies shall have bound us hand and foot? Sir, we are not weak if we make a proper use of those means which the God of nature hath placed in our power. Three millions of people, armed in the holy cause of liberty, and in such a country as that which we possess, are invincible by any force which our enemy can send against us. Besides, sir, we shall not fight our battles alone. There is a just God who presides over the destinies of nations; and who will raise up friends to fight our battles for us. The battle, sir, is not to the strong alone; it is to the vigilant, the active, the brave. Besides, sir, we have no election. If we were base enough to desire it, it is now too late to retire from the contest. There is no retreat but in submission and slavery! Our chains are forged! Their clanking may be heard on the plains of Boston! The war is inevitable²and let it come! I repeat it, sir, let it come.

It is in vain, sir, to extenuate the matter. Gentlemen may cry, Peace, Peace²but there is no peace. The war is actually begun! The next gale that sweeps from the north will bring to our ears the clash of resounding arms! Our brethren are already in the field! Why stand we here idle? What is it that gentlemen wish?

What would they have? Is life so dear, or peace so sweet, as to be purchased at the price of chains and slavery? Forbid it, Almighty God! I know not what course others may take; but as for me, give me liberty or give me death!

Source: Wirt, William. <u>Sketches of the Life and Character of Patrick Henry</u>. (Philadelphia) 1836, as reproduced in <u>The World's Great Speeches</u>, Lewis Copeland and Lawrence W. Lamm, eds., (New York) 1973.

From: P A T R I C K   H E N R Y
BY MOSES COIT TYLER
HOUGHTON MIFFLIN COMPANY
T h e   R i v e r s i d e   P r e s s   C a m b r i d g e   1 8 8 7

CHAPTER II WAS HE ILLITERATE?

Concerning the quality and extent of Patrick Henry's early education, it is perhaps impossible now to speak with entire confidence. On the one hand there seems to have been a tendency, in his own time and since, to overstate his lack of education, and this partly, it may be, from a certain instinctive fascination which one finds in pointing to so dramatic a contrast as that between the sway which the great orator wielded over the minds of other men and the untrained vigor and illiterate spontaneity of his own mind. Then, too, it must be admitted that, whatever early education Patrick Henry may have received, he did, in certain companies and at certain periods of his life, rather too perfectly conceal it under an uncouth garb and manner, and under a pronunciation which, to say the least, was archaic and provincial. Jefferson told Daniel Webster that Patrick Henry's "pronunciation was vulgar and vicious," although, as Jefferson adds, this "was forgotten while he was speaking." Governor John Page "used to relate, on the testimony of his own ears," that Patrick Henry would speak of "the yearth," and of "men's naiteral parts being improved by larnin';" while Spencer Roane mentions his pronunciation of China as "Cheena."

All this, however, it should be noted, does not prove illiteracy. If, indeed, such was his ordinary speech, and not, as some have suggested, a manner adopted on particular occasions for the purpose of identifying himself with the mass of his hearers, the fact is evidence merely that he retained through his mature life, on the one hand, some relics of an old-fashioned good usage, and, on the other, some traces of the brogue of the district in which he was born, just as Edmund Pendleton used to say "scaicely" for scarcely, and as John Taylor, of Caroline, would say "bare" for bar; just as Thomas Chalmers always retained the brogue of Fifeshire, and Thomas Carlyle that of Ecclefechan. Certainly a brogue can never be elegant, but as it has many times coexisted with very high intellectual cultivation, its existence in Patrick Henry does not prove him to have been uncultivated.

Then, too, it must be remembered that he himself had a habit of depreciating his own acquaintance with books, and his own dependence on them. He did this, it would seem, partly from a consciousness that it would only increase his hold on the sympathy and support of the mass of the people of Virginia if they should regard him as absolutely one of themselves, and in no sense raised above them by artificial advantages. Moreover, this habit of self-depreciation would be brought into play when he was in conversation with such professed devourers of books as John Adams and Jefferson, compared with whom he might very properly feel an unfeigned conviction that he was no reader at all,—a conviction in which they would be quite likely to agree with him, and which they would be very likely to express. Thus, John Adams mentions that, in the first intimacy of their friendship begun at the Congress of 1774, the Virginian orator, at his lodgings, confessed one night that, for himself, he had "had no public education;" that at fifteen he had "read Virgil and Livy," but that he had "not looked into a Latin book since." Upon Jefferson, who of course knew Henry far longer and far more closely, the impression of his disconnection from books seems to have been even more decided, especially if we may accept the testimony of Jefferson's old age, when his memory had taken to much stumbling, and his imagination even more to extravagance than in his earlier life. Said Jefferson, in 1824, of his ancient friend: "He was a man of very little knowledge of any sort. He read nothing, and had no books."

On the other hand, there are certain facts concerning Henry's early education and intellectual habits which may be regarded as pretty well established.

Before the age of ten, at a petty neighborhood school, he had got started upon the three primary steps of knowledge. Then, from ten to fifteen, whatever may have been his own irregularity and disinclination, he was member of a home school, under the immediate training of his father and his uncle, both of them good Scotch classical scholars, and one of them at least a proficient in mathematics. No doubt the human mind, especially in its best estate of juvenile vigor and frivolity, has remarkable aptitude for the repulsion of unwelcome knowledge; but it can hardly be said that even Patrick Henry's gift in that direction could have prevented his becoming, under two such masters, tolerably well grounded in Latin, if not in Greek, or that the person who at fifteen is able to read Virgil and Livy, no matter what may be his subsequent neglect of Latin authors, is not already imbued with the essential and indestructible rudiments of the best intellectual culture.

It is this early initiation, on the basis of a drill in Latin, into the art and mystery of expression, which Patrick Henry received from masters so competent and so deeply interested in him, which helps us to understand a certain trait of his, which puzzled Jefferson, and which, without this clue, would certainly be inexplicable. From his first appearance as a speaker to the end of his days, he showed himself to be something more than a declaimer,—indeed, an adept in language. "I have been often astonished," said Jefferson, "at his command of proper language; how he obtained the knowledge of it I never could find out, as he read little, and conversed little with educated men." It is true, probably, that we have no perfect report of any speech he ever made; but even through the obvious imperfections of his reporters there always gleams a certain superiority in diction,—a mastery of the logic and potency of fitting words; such a mastery as genius alone, without special training, cannot account for. Furthermore, we have in the letters of his which survive, and which of course were generally spontaneous and quite unstudied effusions, absolutely authentic and literal examples of his ordinary use of words. Some of these letters will be found in the following pages. Even as manuscripts, I should insist that the letters of Patrick Henry are witnesses to the fact and quality of real intellectual cultivation: these are not the manuscripts of an uneducated person. In penmanship, punctuation, spelling, syntax, they are, upon the whole, rather better than the letters of most of the great actors in our Revolution. But, aside from the mere mechanics of written speech, there is in the diction of Patrick Henry's letters the nameless felicity which, even with great natural endowments, is only communicable by genuine literary culture in some form. Where did Patrick Henry get such literary culture? The question can be answered only by pointing to that painful drill in Latin which the book-hating boy suffered under his uncle and his father, when, to his anguish, Virgil and Livy detained him anon from the true joys of existence.

Wirt seems to have satisfied himself, on evidence carefully gathered from persons who were contemporaries of Patrick Henry, that the latter had received in his youth no mean classical education; but, in the final revision of his book for publication, Wirt abated his statements on that subject, in deference to the somewhat vehement assertions of Jefferson. It may be that, in its present lessened form, Wirt's account of the matter is the more correct one; but this is the proper place in which to mention one bit of direct testimony upon the subject, which, probably, was not known to Wirt. Patrick Henry is said to have told his eldest grandson, Colonel Patrick Henry Fontaine, that he was instructed by his uncle "not only in the catechism, but in the Greek and Latin classics." It may help us to realize something of the moral stamina entering into the training which the unfledged orator thus got that, as he related, his uncle taught him these maxims of conduct: "To be true and just in all my dealings. To bear no malice nor hatred in my heart. To keep my hands from picking and stealing. Not to covet other men's goods; but to learn and labor truly to get my own living, and to do my duty in that state of life unto which it shall please God to call me."

Under such a teacher Patrick Henry was so thoroughly grounded, at least in Latin and Greek grammar, that when, long afterward, his eldest grandson was a student in Hampden-Sidney College, the latter found "his grandfather's examinations of his progress in Greek and Latin" so rigorous that he dreaded them "much more than he did his recitations to his professors." Colonel Fontaine also states that he was present when a certain French visitor, who did not speak English, was introduced to Governor Henry, who did not speak French. During the war of the Revolution and just afterwards a similar embarrassment was not infrequent here in the case of our public men, among whom the study of French had been very uncommon; and for many of them the old colonial habit of fitting boys for college by training them to the colloquial use of Latin proved to be a great convenience. Colonel Fontaine's anecdote implies, what is altogether probable, that Patrick Henry's early drill in Latin had included the ordinary colloquial use of it; for he says that in the case of the visitor in question his grandfather was able, by means of his early stock of Latin words, to carry on the conversation in that language.

This anecdote, implying Patrick Henry's ability to express himself in Latin, I give for what it may be worth. Some will think it incredible, and that impression will be further increased by the fact that Colonel Fontaine names Albert Gallatin as the visitor with whom, on account of his ignorance of English, the conversation was thus carried on in Latin. This, of course, must be a mistake; for, at the time of his first visit to Virginia, Gallatin could speak English very well, so well, in fact, that he went to Virginia expressly as English interpreter to a French gentleman who could not speak our language. However, as, during all that period, Governor Henry had many foreign visitors, Colonel Fontaine, in his subsequent account of that particular visitor, might easily have misplaced the name without thereby discrediting the substance of his narrative. Indeed, the substance of his narrative, namely, that he, Colonel Fontaine, did actually witness, in the case of some foreign visitor, such an exhibition of his grandfather's good early training in Latin, cannot be rejected without an impeachment of the veracity of the narrator, or at least of that of his son, who has recorded the alleged incident. Of course, if that narrative be accepted as substantially true, it will be necessary to conclude that the Jeffersonian tradition of Patrick Henry's illiteracy is, at any rate, far too highly tinted.

Thus far we have been dealing with the question of Patrick Henry's education down to the time of his leaving school, at the age of fifteen. It was not until nine years afterward that he began the study of the law. What is the intellectual record of these nine years? It is obvious that they were years unfavorable to systematic training of any sort, or to any regulated acquisition of knowledge. During all that time in his life, as we now look back upon it, he has for us the aspect of some lawless, unkempt genius, in untoward circumstances, groping in the dark, not without wild joy, towards his inconceivable, true vocation; set to tasks for which he was grotesquely unfit; blundering on from misfortune to misfortune, with an overflow of unemployed energy and vivacity that swept him often into rough fun, into great gusts of innocent riot and horseplay; withal borne along, for many days together, by the mysterious undercurrents of his nature, into that realm of reverie where the soul feeds on immortal fruit and communes with unseen associates, the body meanwhile being left to the semblance of idleness; of all which the man himself might have given this valid justification:—

"I loafe and invite my soul, I lean and loafe at my ease, observing a spear of summer grass."

Nevertheless, these nine years of groping, blundering, and seeming idleness were not without their influence on his intellectual improvement even through direct contact with books. While still a boy in his teens, and put prematurely to uncongenial attempts at shopkeeping and farmkeeping, he at any rate made the great discovery that in books and in the gathering of knowledge from books could be found solace and entertainment; in short, he then acquired a taste for reading. No one pretends that Patrick Henry ever became a bookish person. From the first and always the habit of his mind was that of direct action upon every subject that he had to deal with, through his own reflection, and along the broad primary lines of common sense. There is never in his thought anything subtle or recondite,—no mental movement through the media of books; but there is good evidence for saying that this bewildered and undeveloped youth, drifting about in chaos, did in those days actually get a taste for reading, and that he never lost it. The books which he first read are vaguely described as "a few light and elegant authors," probably in English essays and fiction. As the years passed and the boy's mind matured, he rose to more serious books. He became fond of geography and of history, and he pushed his readings, especially, into the history of Greece and of Rome. He was particularly fascinated by Livy, which he read in the English translation; and then it was, as he himself related it to Judge Hugh Nelson, that he made the rule to read Livy through "once at least in every year during the early part of his life." He read also, it is apparent, the history of England and of the English colonies in America, and especially of his own colony; for the latter finding, no doubt, in Beverley and in the grave and noble pages of Stith, and especially in the colonial charters given by Stith, much material for those incisive opinions which he so early formed as to the rights of the colonies, and as to the barriers to be thrown up against the encroaching authority of the mother country.

There is much contemporaneous evidence to show that Patrick Henry was throughout life a deeply religious person. It certainly speaks well for his intellectual fibre, as well as for his spiritual tendencies, that his favorite book, during the larger part of his life, was "Butler's Analogy," which was first published in the very year in which he was born. It is possible that even during these years of his early manhood he had begun his enduring intimacy with that robust book. Moreover, we can hardly err in saying that he had then also become a steady reader of the English Bible, the diction of which is stamped upon his style as unmistakably as it is upon that of the elder Pitt.

Such, I think it may fairly be said, was Patrick Henry when, at the age of twenty-four, having failed in every other pursuit, he turned for bread to the profession of the law. There is no evidence that either he or any other mortal man was aware of the extraordinary gifts that lay within him for success in that career. Not a scholar surely, not even a considerable miscellaneous reader, he yet had the basis of a good education; he had the habit of reading over and over again a few of the best books; he had a good memory; he had an intellect strong to grasp the great commanding features of any subject; he had a fondness for the study of human nature, and singular proficiency in that branch of science; he had quick and warm sympathies, particularly with persons in trouble,—an invincible propensity to take sides with the under-dog in any fight. Through a long experience in offhand talk with the men whom he had thus far chiefly known in his little provincial world,—with an occasional clergyman, pedagogue, or legislator, small planters and small traders, sportsmen, loafers, slaves and the drivers of slaves, and, more than all, those bucolic Solons of old Virginia, the good-humored, illiterate, thriftless Caucasian consumers of tobacco and whiskey, who, cordially consenting that all the hard work of the world should be done by the children of Ham, were thus left free to commune together in endless debate on the tavern porch or on the shady side of the country store,—young Patrick had learned somewhat of the lawyer's art of putting things; he could make men laugh, could make them serious, could set fire to their enthusiasms. What more he might do with such gifts nobody seems to have guessed; very likely few gave it any thought at all. In that rugged but munificent profession at whose outward gates he then proceeded to knock, it was altogether improbable that he would burden himself with much more of its erudition than was really necessary for a successful general practice in Virginia in his time, or that he would permanently content himself with less.

CHAPTER XVIII THE BATTLE IN VIRGINIA OVER THE NEW CONSTITUTION

The great convention at Philadelphia, after a session of four months, came to the end of its noble labors on the 17th of September, 1787. Washington, who had been not merely its presiding officer but its presiding genius, then hastened back to Mt. Vernon, and, in his great anxiety to win over to the new Constitution the support of his old friend Patrick Henry, he immediately dispatched to him a copy of that instrument, accompanied by a very impressive and conciliatory letter, to which, about three weeks afterwards, was returned the following reply:—

Richmond, October 19, 1787.

Dear Sir,—I was honored by the receipt of your favor, together with a copy of the proposed federal Constitution, a few days ago, for which I beg you to accept my thanks. They are also due to you from me as a citizen, on account of the great fatigue necessarily attending the arduous business of the late convention.

I have to lament that I cannot bring my mind to accord with the proposed Constitution. The concern I feel on this account is really greater than I am able to express. Perhaps mature reflections may furnish me with reasons to change my present sentiments into a conformity with the opinions of those personages for whom I have the highest reverence. Be that as it may, I beg you will be persuaded of the unalterable regard and attachment with which I shall be,

Dear Sir, your obliged and very humble servant,

P. Henry.

Four days before the date of this letter the legislature of Virginia had convened at Richmond for its autumn session, and Patrick Henry had there taken his usual place on the most important committees, and as the virtual director of the thought and work of the House. Much solicitude was felt concerning the course which he might advise the legislature to adopt on the supreme question then before the country,—some persons even fearing that he might try to defeat the new Constitution in Virginia by simply preventing the call of a state convention. Great was Washington's satisfaction on receiving from one of his correspondents in the Assembly, shortly after the session began, this cheerful report:—

"I have not met with one in all my inquiries (and I have made them with great diligence) opposed to it, except Mr. Henry, who I have heard is so, but could only conjecture it from a conversation with him on the subject.... The transmissory note of Congress was before us to-day, when Mr. Henry declared that it transcended our powers to decide on the Constitution, and that it must go before a convention. As it was insinuated he would aim at preventing this, much pleasure was discovered at the declaration."

On the 24th of October, from his place in Congress, Madison sent over to

Jefferson, in Paris, a full account of the results of the Philadelphia convention, and of the public feeling with reference to its work: "My information from Virginia is as yet extremely imperfect.... The part which Mr. Henry will take is unknown here. Much will depend on it. I had taken it for granted, from a variety of circumstances, that he would be in the opposition, and still think that will be the case. There are reports, however, which favor a contrary supposition." But, by the 9th of December, Madison was able to send to Jefferson a further report, which indicated that all doubt respecting the hostile attitude of Patrick Henry was then removed. After mentioning that a majority of the people of Virginia seemed to be in favor of the Constitution, he added: "What change may be produced by the united influence and exertions of Mr. Henry, Mr. Mason, and the governor, with some pretty able auxiliaries, is uncertain.... Mr. Henry is the great adversary who will render the event precarious. He is, I find, with his usual address, working up every possible interest into a spirit of opposition."

Long before the date last mentioned, the legislature had regularly declared for a state convention, to be held at Richmond on the first Monday in June, 1788, then and there to determine whether or not Virginia would accept the new Constitution. In view of that event, delegates were in the mean time to be chosen by the people; and thus, for the intervening months, the fight was to be transferred to the arena of popular debate. In such a contest Patrick Henry, being once aroused, was not likely to take a languid or a hesitating part; and of the importance then attached to the part which he did take, we catch frequent glimpses in the correspondence of the period. Thus, on the 19th of February, 1788, Madison, still at New York, sent this word to Jefferson: "The temper of Virginia, as far as I can learn, has undergone but little change of late. At first, there was an enthusiasm for the Constitution. The tide next took a sudden and strong turn in the opposite direction. The influence and exertions of Mr. Henry, Colonel Mason, and some others, will account for this.... I am told that a very bold language is held by Mr. Henry and some of his partisans." On the 10th of April, Madison, then returned to his home in Virginia, wrote to Edmund Randolph: "The declaration of Henry, mentioned in your letter, is a proof to me that desperate measures will be his game." On the 22d of the same month Madison wrote to Jefferson: "The adversaries take very different grounds of opposition. Some are opposed to the substance of the plan; others, to particular modifications only. Mr. Henry is supposed to aim at disunion." On the 24th of April, Edward Carrington, writing from New York, told Jefferson: "Mr. H. does not openly declare for a dismemberment of the Union, but his arguments in support of his opposition to the Constitution go directly to that issue. He says that three confederacies would be practicable, and better suited to the good of commerce than one." On the 28th of April, Washington wrote to Lafayette on account of the struggle then going forward; and after naming some of the leading champions of the Constitution, he adds sorrowfully: "Henry and Mason are its great adversaries." Finally, as late as on the 12th of June, the Rev. John Blair Smith, at that time president of Hampden-Sidney College, conveyed to Madison, an old college friend, his own deep disapproval of the course which had been pursued by Patrick Henry in the management of the canvass against the Constitution:—

"Before the Constitution appeared, the minds of the people were artfully prepared against it; so that all opposition [to Mr. Henry] at the election of delegates to consider it, was in vain. That gentleman has descended to lower artifices and management on the occasion than I thought him capable of.... If Mr. Innes has shown you a speech of Mr. Henry to his constituents, which I sent him, you will see something of the method he has taken to diffuse his poison.... It grieves me to see such great natural talents abused to such purposes."

On Monday, the 2d of June, 1788, the long-expected convention assembled at Richmond. So great was the public interest in the event that a full delegation was present, even on the first day; and in order to make room for the throngs of citizens from all parts of Virginia and from other States, who had flocked thither to witness the impending battle, it was decided that the convention should hold its meetings in the New Academy, on Shockoe Hill, the largest assembly-room in the city.

Eight States had already adopted the Constitution. The five States which had yet to act upon the question were New Hampshire, Rhode Island, New York, North Carolina, and Virginia. For every reason, the course then to be taken by Virginia would have great consequences. Moreover, since the days of the struggle over independence, no question had so profoundly moved the people of Virginia; none had aroused such hopes and such fears; none had so absorbed the thoughts, or so embittered the relations of men. It is not strange, therefore, that this convention, consisting of one hundred and seventy members, should have been thought to represent, to an unusual degree, the intelligence, the character, the experience, the reputation of the State. Perhaps it would be true to say that, excepting Washington, Jefferson, and Richard Henry Lee, no Virginian of eminence was absent from it.

Furthermore, the line of division, which from the outset parted into two hostile sections these one hundred and seventy Virginians, was something quite unparalleled. In other States it had been noted that the conservative classes, the men of education and of property, of high office, of high social and professional standing, were nearly all on the side of the new Constitution. Such was not the case in Virginia. Of the conservative classes throughout that State, quite as many were against the new Constitution as were in favor of it. Of the four distinguished citizens who had been its governors, since Virginia had assumed the right to elect governors,—Patrick Henry, Jefferson, Nelson, and Harrison,—each in turn had denounced the measure as unsatisfactory and dangerous; while Edmund Randolph, the governor then in office, having attended the great convention at Philadelphia, and having there refused to sign the Constitution, had published an impressive statement of his objections to it, and, for several months thereafter, had been counted among its most formidable opponents. Concerning the attitude of the legal profession,—a profession always inclined to conservatism,—Madison had written to Jefferson: "The general and admiralty courts, with most of the bar, oppose the Constitution." Finally, among Virginians who were at that time particularly honored and trusted for patriotic services during the Revolution, such men as these, Theodoric Bland, William Grayson, John Tyler, Meriwether Smith, James Monroe, George Mason, and Richard Henry Lee, had declared their disapproval of the document.

Nevertheless, within the convention itself, at the opening of the session, it was claimed by the friends of the new government that they then outnumbered their opponents by at least fifty votes. Their great champion in debate was James Madison, who was powerfully assisted, first or last, by Edmund Pendleton, John Marshall, George Nicholas, Francis Corbin, George Wythe, James Innes, General Henry Lee, and especially by that same Governor Randolph who, after denouncing the Constitution for "features so odious" that he could not "agree to it," had finally swung completely around to its support.

Against all this array of genius, learning, character, logical acumen, and eloquence, Patrick Henry held the field as protagonist for twenty-three days,— his chief lieutenants in the fight being Mason, Grayson, and John Dawson, with occasional help from Harrison, Monroe, and Tyler. Upon him alone fell the brunt of the battle. Out of the twenty-three days of that splendid tourney, there were but five days in which he did not take the floor. On each of several days he made three speeches; on one day he made five speeches; on another day eight. In one speech alone, he was on his legs for seven hours. The words of all who had any share in that debate were taken down, according to the imperfect art of the time, by the stenographer, David Robertson, whose reports, however, are said to be little more than a pretty full outline of the speeches actually made: but in the volume which contains these abstracts, one of Patrick Henry's speeches fills eight pages, another ten pages, another sixteen, another twenty-one, another forty; while, in the aggregate, his speeches constitute nearly one quarter of the entire book,—a book of six hundred and sixty-three pages.

Any one who has fallen under the impression, so industriously propagated by the ingenious enmity of Jefferson's old age, that Patrick Henry was a man of but meagre information and of extremely slender intellectual resources, ignorant especially of law, of political science, and of history, totally lacking in logical power and in precision of statement, with nothing to offset these deficiencies excepting a strange gift of overpowering, dithyrambic eloquence, will find it hard, as he turns over the leaves on which are recorded the debates of the Virginia convention, to understand just how such a person could have made the speeches which are there attributed to Patrick Henry, or how a mere rhapsodist could have thus held his ground, in close hand-to-hand combat, for twenty-three days, against such antagonists, on all the difficult subjects of law, political science, and history involved in the Constitution of the United States,— while showing at the same time every quality of good generalship as a tactician and as a party leader. "There has been, I am aware," says an eminent historian of the Constitution, "a modern scepticism concerning Patrick Henry's abilities; but I cannot share it.... The manner in which he carried on the opposition to the Constitution in the convention of Virginia, for nearly a whole month, shows that he possessed other powers besides those of great natural eloquence."

But, now, what were Patrick Henry's objections to the new Constitution?

First of all, let it be noted that his objections did not spring from any hostility to the union of the thirteen States, or from any preference for a separate union of the Southern States. Undoubtedly there had been a time, especially under the provocations connected with the Mississippi business, when he and many other Southern statesmen sincerely thought that there might be no security for their interests even under the Confederation, and that this lack of security would be even more glaring and disastrous under the new Constitution. Such, for example, seems to have been the opinion of Governor Benjamin Harrison, as late as October the 4th, 1787, on which date he thus wrote to Washington: "I cannot divest myself of an opinion that ... if the Constitution is carried into effect, the States south of the Potomac will be little more than appendages to those to the northward of it." It is very probable that this sentence accurately reflects, likewise, Patrick Henry's mood of thought at that time. Nevertheless, whatever may have been his thought under the sectional suspicions and alarms of the preceding months, it is certain that, at the date of the Virginia convention, he had come to see that the thirteen States must, by all means, try to keep together. "I am persuaded," said he, in reply to Randolph, "of what the honorable gentleman says, 'that separate confederacies will ruin us.'" "Sir," he exclaimed on another occasion, "the dissolution of the Union is most abhorrent to my mind. The first thing I have at heart is American liberty; the second thing is American union." Again he protested: "I mean not to breathe the spirit, nor utter the language, of secession."

In the second place, he admitted that there were great defects in the old Confederation, and that those defects ought to be cured by proper amendments, particularly in the direction of greater strength to the federal government. But did the proposed Constitution embody such amendments? On the contrary, that Constitution, instead of properly amending the old Confederation, simply annihilated it, and replaced it by something radically different and radically dangerous.

"The federal convention ought to have amended the old system; for this purpose they were solely delegated; the object of their mission extended to no other consideration." "The distinction between a national government and a confederacy is not sufficiently discerned. Had the delegates who were sent to Philadelphia a power to propose a consolidated government, instead of a confederacy?" "Here is a resolution as radical as that which separated us from Great Britain. It is radical in this transition; our rights and privileges are endangered, and the sovereignty of the States will be relinquished: and cannot we plainly see that this is actually the case? The rights of conscience, trial by jury, liberty of the press, all your immunities and franchises, all pretensions to human rights and privileges, are rendered insecure, if not lost, by this change, so loudly talked of by some, so inconsiderately by others." "A number of characters, of the greatest eminence in this country, object to this government for its consolidating tendency. This is not imaginary. It is a formidable reality. If consolidation proves to be as mischievous to this country as it has been to other countries, what will the poor inhabitants of this country do? This government will operate like an ambuscade. It will destroy the state governments, and swallow the liberties of the people, without giving previous notice. If gentlemen are willing to run the hazard, let them run it; but I shall exculpate myself by my opposition and monitory warnings within these walls."

But, in the third place, besides transforming the old confederacy into a centralized and densely consolidated government, and clothing that government with enormous powers over States and over individuals, what had this new Constitution provided for the protection of States and of individuals? Almost nothing. It had created a new and a tremendous power over us; it had failed to cover us with any shield, or to interpose any barrier, by which, in case of need, we might save ourselves from the wanton and fatal exercise of that power. In short, the new Constitution had no bill of rights. But "a bill of rights," he declared, is "indispensably necessary."

"A general positive provision should be inserted in the new system, securing to the States and the people every right which was not conceded to the general government." "I trust that gentlemen, on this occasion, will see the great objects of religion, liberty of the press, trial by jury, interdiction of cruel punishments, and every other sacred right, secured, before they agree to that paper." "Mr. Chairman, the necessity of a bill of rights appears to me to be greater in this government than ever it was in any government before. I have observed already that the sense of European nations, and particularly Great Britain, is against the construction of rights being retained which are not expressly relinquished. I repeat, that all nations have adopted the construction, that all rights not expressly and unequivocally reserved to the people are impliedly and incidentally relinquished to rulers, as necessarily inseparable from delegated powers.... Let us consider the sentiments which have been entertained by the people of America on this subject. At the Revolution, it must be admitted that it was their sense to set down those great rights which ought, in all countries, to be held inviolable and sacred. Virginia did so, we all remember. She made a compact to reserve, expressly, certain rights.... She most cautiously and guardedly reserved and secured those invaluable, inestimable rights and privileges which no people, inspired with the least glow of patriotic liberty, ever did, or ever can, abandon. She is called upon now to abandon them, and dissolve that compact which secured them to her.... Will she do it? This is the question. If you intend to reserve your unalienable rights, you must have the most express stipulation; for, if implication be allowed, you are ousted of those rights. If the people do not think it necessary to reserve them, they will be supposed to be given up.... If you give up these powers, without a bill of rights, you will exhibit the most absurd thing to mankind that ever the world saw,—a government that has abandoned all its powers,—the powers of direct taxation, the sword, and the purse. You have disposed of them to Congress, without a bill of rights, without check, limitation, or control. And still you have checks and guards; still you keep barriers—pointed where? Pointed against your weakened, prostrated, enervated, state government! You have a bill of rights to defend you against the state government—which is bereaved of all power, and yet you have none against Congress—though in full and exclusive possession of all power. You arm yourselves against the weak and defenceless, and expose yourselves naked to the armed and powerful. Is not this a conduct of unexampled absurdity?"

Again and again, in response to his demand for an express assertion, in the instrument itself, of the rights of individuals and of States, he was told that every one of those rights was secured, since it was naturally and fairly implied. "Even say," he rejoined, "it is a natural implication,—why not give us a right … in express terms, in language that could not admit of evasions or subterfuges? If they can use implication for us, they can also use implication against us. We are giving power; they are getting power; judge, then, on which side the implication will be used." "Implication is dangerous, because it is unbounded; if it be admitted at all, and no limits prescribed, it admits of the utmost extension." "The existence of powers is sufficiently established. If we trust our dearest rights to implication, we shall be in a very unhappy situation."

Then, in addition to his objections to the general character of the Constitution, namely, as a consolidated government, unrestrained by an express guarantee of rights, he applied his criticisms in great detail, and with merciless rigor, to each department of the proposed government,—the legislative, the executive, and the judicial; and with respect to each one of these he insisted that its intended functions were such as to inspire distrust and alarm. Of course, we cannot here follow this fierce critic of the Constitution into all the detail of his criticisms; but, as a single example, we may cite a portion of his assault upon the executive department,—an assault, as will be seen, far better suited to the political apprehensions of his own time than of ours:—

"The Constitution is said to have beautiful features; but when I come to examine these features, sir, they appear to me horribly frightful. Among other deformities, it has an awful squinting; it squints towards monarchy. And does not this raise indignation in the breast of every true American? Your president may easily become king…. Where are your checks in this government? Your strongholds will be in the hands of your enemies. It is on a supposition that your American governors shall be honest, that all the good qualities of this government are founded; but its defective and imperfect construction puts it in their power to perpetrate the worst of mischiefs, should they be bad men. And, sir, would not all the world, from the eastern to the western hemispheres, blame our distracted folly in resting our rights upon the contingency of our rulers being good or bad? Show me that age and country where the rights and liberties of the people were placed on the sole chance of their rulers being good men, without a consequent loss of liberty…. If your American chief be a man of ambition and abilities, how easy is it for him to render himself absolute! The army is in his hands; and if he be a man of address, it will be attached to him, and it will be the subject of long meditation with him to seize the first auspicious moment to accomplish his design. And, sir, will the American spirit solely relieve you when this happens? I would rather infinitely—and I am sure most of this convention are of the same opinion—have a king, lords, and commons, than a government so replete with such insupportable evils. If we make a king, we may prescribe the rules by which he shall rule his people, and interpose such checks as shall prevent him from infringing them; but the president, in the field, at the head of his army, can prescribe the terms on which he shall reign master, so far that it will puzzle any American ever to get his neck from under the galling yoke…. Will not the recollection of his crimes teach him to make one bold push for the American throne? Will not the immense difference between being master of everything, and being ignominiously tried and punished, powerfully excite him to make this bold push? But, sir, where is the existing force to punish him? Can he not, at the head of his army, beat down every opposition? Away with your president! we shall have a king. The army will salute him monarch. Your militia will leave you, and assist in making him king, and fight against you. And what have you to oppose this force? What will then become of you and your rights? Will not absolute despotism ensue?"

Without reproducing here, in further detail, Patrick Henry's objections to the new Constitution, it may now be stated that they all sprang from a single idea, and all revolved about that idea, namely, that the new plan of government, as it then stood, seriously endangered the rights and liberties of the people of the several States. And in holding this opinion he was not at all peculiar. Very many of the ablest and noblest statesmen of the time shared it with him. Not to name again his chief associates in Virginia, nor to cite the language of such men as Burke and Rawlins Lowndes, of South Carolina; as Timothy Bloodworth, of North Carolina; as Samuel Chase and Luther Martin, of Maryland; as George Clinton, of New York; as Samuel Adams, John Hancock, and Elbridge Gerry, of Massachusetts; as Joshua Atherton, of New Hampshire, it may sufficiently put us into the tone of contemporary opinion upon the subject, to recall certain grave words of Jefferson, who, watching the whole scene from the calm distance of Paris, thus wrote on the 2d of February, 1788, to an American friend:—

"I own it astonishes me to find such a change wrought in the opinions of our countrymen since I left them, as that three fourths of them should be contented to live under a system which leaves to their governors the power of taking from them the trial by jury in civil cases, freedom of religion, freedom of the press, freedom of commerce, the habeas corpus laws, and of yoking them with a standing army. That is a degeneracy in the principles of liberty, to which I had given four centuries, instead of four years."

Holding such objections to the proposed Constitution, what were Patrick Henry and his associates in the Virginia convention to do? Were they to reject the measure outright? Admitting that it had some good features, they yet thought that the best course to be taken by Virginia would be to remit the whole subject to a new convention of the States,—a convention which, being summoned after a year or more of intense and universal discussion, would thus represent the later, the more definite, and the more enlightened desires of the American people. But despairing of this, Patrick Henry and his friends concentrated all their forces upon this single and clear line of policy: so to press their objections to the Constitution as to induce the convention, not to reject it, but to postpone its adoption until they could refer to the other States in the American confederacy the following momentous proposition, namely, "a declaration of rights, asserting, and securing from encroachment, the great principles of civil and religious liberty, and the undeniable rights of the people, together with amendments to the most exceptionable parts of the said constitution of government."

Such, then, was the real question over which in that assemblage, from the first day to the last, the battle raged. The result of the battle was reached on

Wednesday, the 25th of June; and that result was a victory for immediate adoption, but by a majority of only ten votes, instead of the fifty votes that were claimed for it at the beginning of the session. Moreover, even that small majority for immediate adoption was obtained only by the help, first, of a preamble solemnly affirming it to be the understanding of Virginia in this act that it retained every power not expressly granted to the general government; and, secondly, of a subsidiary resolution promising to recommend to Congress "whatsoever amendments may be deemed necessary."

Just before the decisive question was put, Patrick Henry, knowing that the result would be against him, and knowing, also, from the angry things uttered within that House and outside of it, that much solicitude was abroad respecting the course likely to be taken by the defeated party, then and there spoke these noble words:—

"I beg pardon of this House for having taken up more time than came to my share, and I thank them for the patience and polite attention with which I have been heard. If I shall be in the minority, I shall have those painful sensations which arise from a conviction of being overpowered in a good cause. Yet I will be a peaceable citizen. My head, my hand, and my heart shall be at liberty to retrieve the loss of liberty, and remove the defects of that system in a constitutional way. I wish not to go to violence, but will wait, with hopes that the spirit which predominated in the Revolution is not yet gone, nor the cause of those who are attached to the Revolution yet lost. I shall therefore patiently wait in expectation of seeing that government changed, so as to be compatible with the safety, liberty, and happiness of the people."

Those words of the great Virginian leader proved to be a message of reassurance to many an anxious citizen, in many a State,—not least so to that great citizen who, from the slopes of Mount Vernon, was then watching, night and day, for signs of some abatement in the storm of civil discord. Those words, too, have, in our time, won for the orator who spoke them the deliberate, and the almost lyrical, applause of the greatest historian who has yet laid hand on the story of the Constitution: "Henry showed his genial nature, free from all malignity. He was like a billow of the ocean on the first bright day after the storm, dashing itself against the rocky cliff, and then, sparkling with light, retreating to its home."

Long after the practical effects of the Virginia convention of 1788 had been merged in the general political life of the country, that convention was still proudly remembered for the magnificent exertions of intellectual power, and particularly of eloquence, which it had called forth. So lately as the year 1857, there was still living a man who, in his youth, had often looked in upon that famous convention, and whose enthusiasm, in recalling its great scenes, was not to be chilled even by the frosts of his ninety winters:—

"The impressions made by the powerful arguments of Madison and the overwhelming eloquence of Henry can never fade from my mind. I thought them almost supernatural. They seemed raised up by Providence, each in his way, to produce great results: the one by his grave, dignified, and irresistible arguments to convince and enlighten mankind; the other, by his brilliant and enrapturing eloquence to lead whithersoever he would."

Those who had heard Patrick Henry on the other great occasions of his career were ready to say that his eloquence in the convention of 1788 was, upon the whole, fully equal to anything ever exhibited by him in any other place. The official reports of his speeches in that assemblage were always declared to be inferior in "strength and beauty" to those actually made by him there. "In forming an estimate of his eloquence," says one gentleman who there heard him, "no reliance can be placed on the printed speeches. No reporter whatever could take down what he actually said; and if he could, it would fall far short of the original."

In his arguments against the Constitution Patrick Henry confined himself to no systematic order. The convention had indeed resolved that the document should be discussed, clause by clause, in a regular manner; but in spite of the complaints and reproaches of his antagonists, he continually broke over all barriers, and delivered his "multiform and protean attacks" in such order as suited the workings of his own mind.

In the course of that long and eager controversy, he had several passages of sharp personal collision with his opponents, particularly with Governor Randolph, whose vacillating course respecting the Constitution had left him exposed to the most galling comments, and who on one occasion, in his anguish, turned upon Patrick Henry with the exclamation: "I find myself attacked in the most illiberal manner by the honorable gentleman. I disdain his aspersions and his insinuations. His asperity is warranted by no principle of parliamentary decency, nor compatible with the least shadow of friendship; and if our friendship must fall, let it fall, like Lucifer, never to rise again." Like all very eloquent men, he was taunted, of course, for having more eloquence than logic; for "his declamatory talents;" for his "vague discourses and mere sports of fancy;" for discarding "solid argument;" and for "throwing those bolts" which he had "so peculiar a dexterity at discharging." On one occasion, old General Adam Stephen tried to burlesque the orator's manner of speech; on another occasion, that same petulant warrior bluntly told Patrick that if he did "not like this government," he might "go and live among the Indians," and even offered to facilitate the orator's self-expatriation among the savages: "I know of several nations that live very happily; and I can furnish him with a vocabulary of their language."

Knowing, as he did, every passion and prejudice of his audience, he adopted, it appears, almost every conceivable method of appeal. "The variety of arguments," writes one witness, "which Mr. Henry generally presented in his speeches, addressed to the capacities, prejudices, and individual interests of his hearers, made his speeches very unequal. He rarely made in that convention a speech which Quintilian would have approved. If he soared at times, like the eagle, and seemed like the bird of Jove to be armed with thunder, he did not disdain to stoop like the hawk to seize his prey,—but the instant that he had done it, rose in pursuit of another quarry."

Perhaps the most wonderful example of his eloquence, if we may judge by contemporary descriptions, was that connected with the famous scene of the thunder-storm, on Tuesday, the 24th of June, only one day before the decisive vote was taken. The orator, it seems, had gathered up all his forces for what might prove to be his last appeal against immediate adoption, and was portraying the disasters which the new system of government, unless amended, was to bring upon his countrymen, and upon all mankind: "I see the awful immensity of the dangers with which it is pregnant. I see it. I feel it. I see beings of a higher order anxious concerning our decision. When I see beyond the horizon that bounds human eyes, and look at the final consummation of all human things, and see those intelligent beings which inhabit the ethereal mansions reviewing the political decisions and revolutions which, in the progress of time, will happen in America, and the consequent happiness or misery of mankind, I am led to believe that much of the account, on one side or the other, will depend on what we now decide. Our own happiness alone is not affected by the event. All nations are interested in the determination. We have it in our power to secure the happiness of one half of the human race. Its adoption may involve the misery of the other hemisphere." Thus far the stenographer had proceeded, when he suddenly stopped, and placed within brackets the following note: "[Here a violent storm arose, which put the House in such disorder, that Mr. Henry was obliged to conclude.]" But the scene which is thus quietly despatched by the official reporter of the convention was again and again described, by many who were witnesses of it, as something most sublime and even appalling. After having delineated with overpowering vividness the calamities which were likely to befall mankind from their adoption of the proposed frame of government, the orator, it is said, as if wielding an enchanter's wand, suddenly enlarged the arena of the debate and the number of his auditors; for, peering beyond the veil which shuts in mortal sight, and pointing "to those celestial beings who were hovering over the scene," he addressed to them "an invocation that made every nerve shudder with supernatural horror, when, lo! a storm at that instant rose, which shook the whole building, and the spirits whom he had called seemed to have come at his bidding. Nor did his eloquence, or the storm, immediately cease; but availing himself of the incident, with a master's art, he seemed to mix in the fight of his ethereal auxiliaries, and, 'rising on the wings of the tempest, to seize upon the artillery of heaven, and direct its fiercest thunders against the heads of his adversaries.' The scene became insupportable; and the House rose without the formality of adjournment, the members rushing from their seats with precipitation and confusion."

CHAPTER XIX THE AFTER-FIGHT FOR AMENDMENTS

Thus, on the question of adopting the new Constitution, the fight was over; but on the question of amending that Constitution, now that it had been adopted, the fight, of course, was only just begun.

For how could this new Constitution be amended? A way was provided,—but an extremely strait and narrow way. No amendment whatsoever could become valid until it had been accepted by three fourths of the States; and no amendment could be submitted to the States for their consideration until it had first been approved, either by two thirds of both houses of Congress, or else by a majority of a convention specially called by Congress at the request of two thirds of the States.

Clearly, the framers of the Constitution intended that the supreme law of the land, when once agreed to, should have within it a principle of fixedness almost invincible. At any rate, the process by which alone alterations can be made, involves so wide an area of territory, so many distinct groups of population, and is withal, in itself, so manifold and complex, so slow, and so liable to entire stoppage, that any proposition looking toward change must inevitably perish long before reaching the far-away goal of final endorsement, unless that proposition be really impelled by a public demand not only very energetic and persistent, but well-nigh universal. Indeed, the constitutional provision for amendments seemed, at that time, to many, to be almost a constitutional prohibition of amendments.

It was, in part, for this very reason that Patrick Henry had urged that those amendments of the Constitution which, in his opinion, were absolutely necessary, should be secured before its adoption, and not be left to the doubtful chance of their being obtained afterward, as the result of a process ingeniously contrived, as it were, to prevent their being obtained at all. But at the close of that June day on which he and his seventy-eight associates walked away from the convention wherein, on this very proposition, they had just been voted down, how did the case stand? The Constitution, now become the supreme law of the land, was a Constitution which, unless amended, would, as they sincerely believed, effect the political ruin of the American people. As good citizens, as good men, what was left for them to do? They had fought hard to get the Constitution amended before adoption. They had failed. They must now fight hard to get it amended after adoption. Disastrous would it be, to assume that the needed amendments would now be carried at any rate. True, the Virginia convention, like the conventions of several other States, had voted to recommend amendments. But the hostility to amendments, as Patrick Henry believed, was too deeply rooted to yield to mere recommendations. The necessary amendments would not find their way through all the hoppers and tubes and valves of the enormous mill erected within the Constitution, unless forced onward by popular agitation,—and by popular agitation widespread, determined, vehement, even alarming. The powerful enemies of amendments must be convinced that, until amendments were carried through that mill, there would be no true peace or content among the surrounding inhabitants.

This gives us the clew to the policy steadily and firmly pursued by Patrick Henry as a party leader, from June, 1788, until after the ratification of the first ten amendments, on the 15th of December, 1791. It was simply a strategic policy dictated by his honest view of the situation; a bold, manly, patriotic policy; a policy, however, which was greatly misunderstood, and grossly misrepresented, at the time; a policy, too, which grieved the heart of Washington, and for several years raised between him and his ancient friend the one cloud of distrust that ever cast a shadow upon their intercourse.

In fact, at the very opening of the Virginia convention, and in view of the possible defeat of his demand for amendments, Patrick Henry had formed a clear outline of this policy, even to the extent of organizing throughout the State local societies for stirring up, and for keeping up, the needed agitation. All this is made evident by an important letter written by him to General John Lamb of New York, and dated at Richmond, June 9, 1788,—when the convention had been in session just one week. In this letter, after some preliminary words, he says:—

It is matter of great consolation to find that the sentiments of a vast majority of Virginians are in unison with those of our Northern friends. I am satisfied four fifths of our inhabitants are opposed to the new scheme of government. Indeed, in the part of this country lying south of James River, I am confident, nine tenths are opposed to it. And yet, strange as it may seem, the numbers in convention appear equal on both sides: so that the majority, which way soever it goes, will be small. The friends and seekers of power have, with their usual subtilty, wriggled themselves into the choice of the people, by assuming shapes as various as the faces of the men they address on such occasions.

If they shall carry their point, and preclude previous amendments, which we have ready to offer, it will become highly necessary to form the society you mention. Indeed, it appears the only chance for securing a remnant of those invaluable rights which are yielded by the new plan. Colonel George Mason has agreed to act as chairman of our republican society. His character I need not describe. He is every way fit; and we have concluded to send you by Colonel Oswald a copy of the Bill of Rights, and of the particular amendments we intend to propose in our convention. The fate of them is altogether uncertain; but of that you will be informed. To assimilate our views on this great subject is of the last moment; and our opponents expect much from our dissension. As we see the danger, I think it is easily avoided.

I can assure you that North Carolina is more decidedly opposed to the new government than Virginia. The people there seem rife for hazarding all, before they submit. Perhaps the organization of our system may be so contrived as to include lesser associations dispersed throughout the State. This will remedy in some degree the inconvenience arising from our dispersed situation. Colonel Oswald's short stay here prevents my saying as much on the subject as I could otherwise have done. And after assuring you of my ardent wishes for the happiness of our common country, and the best interests of humanity, I beg leave to subscribe myself, with great respect and regard,

Sir, your obedient, humble servant, P. Henry.

On the 27th of June, within a few hours, very likely, after the final adjournment of the convention, Madison hastened to report to Washington the great and exhilarating result, but with this anxious and really unjust surmise respecting the course then to be pursued by Patrick Henry:—

"Mr. H——y declared, previous to the final question, that although he should submit as a quiet citizen, he should seize the first moment that offered for shaking off the yoke in a constitutional way. I suspect the plan will be to encourage two thirds of the legislatures in the task of undoing the work; or to get a Congress appointed in the first instance that will commit suicide on their own authority."

At the same sitting, probably, Madison sent off to Hamilton, at New York, another report, in which his conjecture as to Patrick Henry's intended policy is thus stated:—

"I am so uncharitable as to suspect that the ill-will to the Constitution will produce every peaceable effort to disgrace and destroy it. Mr. Henry declared ... that he should wait with impatience for the favorable moment of regaining, in a constitutional way, the lost liberties of his country."

Two days afterward, by which time, doubtless, Madison's letter had reached Mount Vernon, Washington wrote to Benjamin Lincoln of Massachusetts, respecting the result of the convention:—

"Our accounts from Richmond are that ... the final decision exhibited a solemn scene, and that there is every reason to expect a perfect acquiescence therein by the minority. Mr. Henry, the great leader of it, has signified that, though he can never be reconciled to the Constitution in its present form, and shall give it every constitutional opposition in his power, yet he will submit to it peaceably."

Thus, about the end of June, 1788, there came down upon the fierce political strife in Virginia a lull, which lasted until the 20th of October, at which time the legislature assembled for its autumnal session. Meantime, however, the convention of New York had adopted the Constitution, but after a most bitter fight, and by a majority of only three votes, and only in consequence of the pledge that every possible effort should be made to obtain speedily those great amendments that were at last called for by a determined public demand. One of the efforts contemplated by the New York convention took the form of a circular letter to the governors of the several States, urging almost pathetically that "effectual measures be immediately taken for calling a convention" to propose those amendments which are necessary for allaying "the apprehensions and discontents" then so prevalent.

This circular letter "rekindled," as Madison then wrote to Jefferson, "an ardor among the opponents of the federal Constitution for an immediate revision of it by another general convention, ... Mr. Henry and his friends in Virginia enter with great zeal into the scheme." In a letter written by Washington, nearly a month before the meeting of the legislature, it is plainly indicated that his mind was then grievously burdened by the anxieties of the situation, and that he was disposed to put the very worst construction upon the expected conduct of Patrick Henry and his party in the approaching session:—

[Pg 346]

"Their expedient will now probably be an attempt to procure the election of so many of their own junto under the new government, as, by the introduction of local and embarrassing disputes, to impede or frustrate its operation.... I assure you I am under painful apprehensions from the single circumstance of Mr. H. having the whole game to play in the Assembly of this State; and the effect it may have in others should be counteracted if possible."

No sooner had the Assembly met, than Patrick Henry's ascendency became apparent. His sway over that body was such that it was described as "omnipotent." And by the time the session had been in progress not quite a month, Washington informed Madison that "the accounts from Richmond" were "very unpropitious to federal measures." "In one word," he added, "it is said that the edicts of Mr. H. are enregistered with less opposition in the Virginia Assembly than those of the grand monarch by his parliaments. He has only to say, Let this be law, and it is law." Within ten days from the opening of the session, the House showed its sensitive response to Patrick Henry's leadership by adopting a series of resolutions, the chief purpose of which was to ask Congress to call immediately a national convention for proposing to the States the required amendments. In the debate on the subject, he is said to have declared "that he should oppose every measure tending to the organization of the government, unless accompanied with measures for the amendment of the Constitution."

Some phrases in one of his resolutions were most offensive to those members of the House who had "befriended the new Constitution," and who, by implication at least, were held forth as "betrayers of the dearest rights of the people." "If Mr. Henry pleases," so wrote a correspondent of Washington, "he will carry the resolution in its present terms, than which none, in my opinion, can be more exceptionable or inflammatory; though, as he is sometimes kind and condescending, he may perhaps be induced to alter it."

In accordance with these resolutions, a formal application to Congress for a national convention was prepared by Patrick Henry, and adopted by the House on the 14th of November. Every word of that document deserves now to be read, as his own account of the spirit and purpose of a measure then and since then so profoundly and so cruelly misinterpreted:—

"The good people of this commonwealth, in convention assembled, having ratified the Constitution submitted to their consideration, this legislature has, in conformity to that act, and the resolutions of the United States in Congress assembled to them transmitted, thought proper to make the arrangements that were *necessary* for carrying it into effect. Having thus shown themselves obedient to the voice of their constituents, all

America will find that, so far as it depends on them, that plan of government will be carried into immediate operation.

"But the sense of the people of Virginia would be but in part complied with, and but little regarded, if we went no further. In the very moment of adoption, and coeval with the ratification of the new plan of government, the general voice of the convention of this State pointed to objects no less interesting to the people we represent, and equally entitled to your attention. At the same time that, from motives of affection for our sister States, the convention yielded their assent to the ratification, they gave the most unequivocal proofs that they dreaded its operation under the present form.

"In acceding to a government under this impression, painful must have been the prospect, had they not derived consolation from a full expectation of its imperfections being speedily amended. In this resource, therefore, they placed their confidence,—a confidence that will continue to support them whilst they have reason to believe they have not calculated upon it in vain.

"In making known to you the objections of the people of this Commonwealth to the new plan of government, we deem it unnecessary to enter into a particular detail of its defects, which they consider as involving all the great and unalienable rights of freemen: for their sense on this subject, we refer you to the proceedings of their late convention, and the sense of this General Assembly, as expressed in their resolutions of the   day of   .

"We think proper, however, to declare that in our opinion, as those objections were not founded in speculative theory, but deduced from principles which have been established by the melancholy example of other nations, in different ages, so they will never be removed until the cause itself shall cease to exist. The sooner, therefore, the public apprehensions are quieted, and the government is possessed of the confidence of the people, the more salutary will be its operations, and the longer its duration.

"The cause of amendments we consider as a common cause; and since concessions have been made from political motives, which we conceive may endanger the republic, we trust that a commendable zeal will be shown for obtaining those provisions which, experience has taught us, are necessary to secure from danger the unalienable rights of human nature.

"The anxiety with which our countrymen press for the accomplishment of this important end, will ill admit of delay. The slow forms of congressional discussion and recommendation, if indeed they should ever agree to any change, would, we fear, be less certain of success. Happily for their wishes, the Constitution hath presented an alternative, by admitting the submission to a convention of the States. To this, therefore, we resort, as the source from whence they are to derive relief from their present apprehensions. We do, therefore, in behalf of our constituents, in the most earnest and solemn manner, make this application to Congress, that a convention be immediately called, of deputies from the several States, with full power to take into their consideration the defects of this Constitution, that have been suggested by the state conventions, and report such amendments thereto, as they shall find best suited to promote our common interests, and secure to ourselves and our latest posterity the great and unalienable rights of mankind."

Such was the purpose, such was the temper, of Virginia's appeal, addressed to Congress, and written by Patrick Henry, on behalf of immediate measures for curing the supposed defects of the Constitution. Was it not likely that this appeal would be granted? One grave doubt haunted the mind of Patrick Henry. If, in the elections for senators and representatives then about to occur in the several States, very great care was not taken, it might easily happen that a majority of the members of Congress would be composed of men who would obstruct, and perhaps entirely defeat, the desired amendments. With the view of doing his part towards the prevention of such a result, he determined that both the senators from Virginia, and as many as possible of its representatives, should be persons who could be trusted to help, and not to hinder, the great project.

Accordingly, when the day came for the election of senators by the Assembly of Virginia, he just stood up in his place and named "Richard Henry Lee and William Grayson, Esquires," as the two men who ought to be elected as senators; and, furthermore, he named James Madison as the one man who ought not to be elected as senator. Whereupon the vote was taken; "and after some time," as the journal expresses it, the committee to examine the ballot-boxes "returned into the House, and reported that they had ... found a majority of votes in favor of Richard Henry Lee and William Grayson, Esquires." On the 8th of December, 1788, just one month afterward, Madison himself, in a letter to Jefferson, thus alluded to the incident: "They made me a candidate for the Senate, for which I had not allotted my pretensions. The attempt was defeated by Mr. Henry, who is omnipotent in the present legislature, and who added to the expedients common on such occasions a public philippic against my federal principles."

Virginia's delegation in the Senate was thus made secure. How about her delegation in the lower house? That, also, was an affair to be sharply looked to. Above all things, James Madison, as the supposed foe of amendments, was to be prevented, if possible, from winning an election. Therefore the committee of the House of Delegates, which was appointed for the very purpose, among other things, of dividing the State into its ten congressional districts, so carved out those districts as to promote the election of the friends of the good cause, and especially to secure, as was hoped, the defeat of its great enemy. Of this committee Patrick Henry was not a member; but as a majority of its members were known to be his devoted followers, very naturally upon him, at the time, was laid the burden of the blame for practising this ignoble device in politics,—a device which, when introduced into Massachusetts several years afterward, also by a Revolutionary father, came to be christened with the satiric name of "gerrymandering." Surely it was a rare bit of luck, in the case of Patrick Henry, that the wits of Virginia did not anticipate the wits of Massachusetts by describing this trick as "henrymandering;" and that he thus narrowly escaped the ugly immortality of having his name handed down from age to age in the coinage of a base word which should designate a base thing,—one of the favorite, shabby manœuvres of less scrupulous American politicians.

Thus, however, within four weeks from the opening of the session, he had succeeded in pressing through the legislature, in the exact form he wished, all these measures for giving effect to Virginia's demand upon Congress for amendments. This being accomplished, he withdrew from the service of the House for the remainder of the session, probably on account of the great urgency of his professional engagements at that time. The journal of the House affords us no trace of his presence there after the 18th of November; and although the legislature continued in session until the 13th of December, its business did not digress beyond local topics. To all these facts, rather bitter allusion is made in a letter to the governor of New Hampshire, written from Mount Vernon, on the 31st of January, 1789, by the private secretary of Washington, Tobias Lear, who thus reflected, no doubt, the mood of his chief:—

"Mr. Henry, the leader of the opposition in this State, finding himself beaten off the ground by fair argument in the state convention, and outnumbered upon the important question, collected his whole strength, and pointed his whole force against the government, in the Assembly. He here met with but a feeble opposition.... He led on his almost unresisted phalanx, and planted the standard of hostility upon the very battlements of federalism. In plain English, he ruled a majority of the Assembly; and his edicts were registered by that body with less opposition than those of the Grand Monarque have met with from his parliaments. He chose the two senators.... He divided the State into districts, ... taking care to arrange matters so as to have the county, of which Mr. Madison is an inhabitant, thrown into a district of which a majority were supposed to be unfriendly to the government, and by that means exclude him from the representative body in Congress. He wrote the answer to Governor Clinton's letter, and likewise the circular letter to the executives of the several States.... And after he had settled everything relative to the government wholly, I suppose, to his satisfaction, he mounted his horse and rode home, leaving the little business of the State to be done by anybody who chose to give themselves the trouble of attending to it."

How great was the effect of these strategic measures, forced by Patrick Henry through the legislature of Virginia in the autumn of 1788, was not apparent, of course, until after the organization of the first Congress of the United States, in the spring of 1789. Not until the 5th of May could time be found by that body for paying the least attention to the subject of amendments. On that day Theodoric Bland, from Virginia, presented to the House of Representatives the solemn application of his State for a new convention; and, after some discussion, this document was entered on the journals of the House. The subject was then dropped until the 8th of June, when Madison, who had been elected to Congress in spite of Patrick Henry, and who had good reason to know how dangerous it would be for Congress to trifle with the popular demand for amendments, succeeded, against much opposition, in getting the House to devote that day to a preliminary discussion of the business. It was again laid aside for nearly six weeks, and again got a slight hearing on the 21st of July. On the 13th of August it was once more brought to the reluctant attention of the House, and then proved the occasion of a debate which lasted until the

24th of that month, when the House finished its work on the subject, and sent up to the Senate seventeen articles of amendment. Only twelve of these articles succeeded in passing the Senate; and of these twelve, only ten received from the States that approval which was necessary to their ratification. This was obtained on the 15th of December, 1791.

The course thus taken by Congress, in itself proposing amendments, was not at the time pleasing to the chiefs of that party which, in the several States, had been clamorous for amendments. These men, desiring more radical changes in the Constitution than could be expected from Congress, had set their hearts on a new convention,—which, undoubtedly, had it been called, would have reconstructed, from top to bottom, the work done by the convention of 1787. Yet it should be noticed that the ten amendments, thus obtained under the initiative of Congress, embodied "nearly every material change suggested by Virginia;" and that it was distinctly due, in no small degree, to the bitter and implacable urgency of the popular feeling in Virginia, under the stimulus of Patrick Henry's leadership, that Congress was induced by Madison to pay any attention to the subject. In the matter of amendments, therefore, Patrick Henry and his party did not get all that they demanded, nor in the way that they demanded; but even so much as they did get, they would not then have got at all, had they not demanded more, and demanded more, also, through the channel of a new convention, the dread of which, it is evident, drove Madison and his brethren in Congress into the prompt concession of amendments which they themselves did not care for. Those amendments were really a tub to the whale; but then that tub would not have been thrown overboard at all, had not the whale been there, and very angry, and altogether too troublesome with his foam-compelling tail, and with that huge head of his which could batter as well as spout.

CHAPTER XIII FIRST GOVERNOR OF THE STATE OF VIRGINIA

On Friday, the 5th of July, 1776, Patrick Henry took the oath of office, and entered upon his duties as governor of the commonwealth of Virginia. The salary attached to the position was fixed at one thousand pounds sterling for the year; and the governor was invited to take up his residence in the palace at Williamsburg. No one had resided in the palace since Lord Dunmore had fled from it; and the people of Virginia could hardly fail to note the poetic retribution whereby the very man whom, fourteen months before, Lord Dunmore had contemptuously denounced as "a certain Patrick Henry of Hanover County," should now become Lord Dunmore's immediate successor in that mansion of state, and should be able, if he chose, to write proclamations against Lord Dunmore upon the same desk on which Lord Dunmore had so recently written the proclamation against himself.

Among the first to bring their congratulations to the new governor, were his devoted friends, the first and second regiments of Virginia, who told him that they viewed "with the sincerest sentiments of respect and joy" his accession to the highest office in the State, and who gave to him likewise this affectionate assurance: "our hearts are willing, and arms ready, to maintain your authority as chief magistrate." On the 29th of July, the erratic General Charles Lee, who was then in Charleston, sent on his congratulations in a letter amusing for its tart cordiality and its peppery playfulness:—

"I most sincerely congratulate you on the noble conduct of your countrymen; and I congratulate your country on having citizens deserving of the high honor to which you are exalted. For the being elected to the first magistracy of a free people is certainly the pinnacle of human glory; and I am persuaded that they could not have made a happier choice. Will you excuse me,—but I am myself so extremely democratical, that I think it a fault in your constitution that the governor should be eligible for three years successively. It appears to me that a government of three years may furnish an opportunity of acquiring a very dangerous influence. But this is not the worst.... A man who is fond of office, and has his eye upon reëlection, will be courting favor and popularity at the expense of his duty.... There is a barbarism crept in among us that extremely shocks me: I mean those tinsel epithets with which (I come in for my share) we are so beplastered,—'his excellency,' and 'his honor,' 'the honorable president of the honorable congress,' or 'the honorable convention.' This fulsome, nauseating cant may be well enough adapted to barbarous monarchies, or to gratify the adulterated pride of the 'magnifici' in pompous aristocracies; but in a great, free, manly, equal commonwealth, it is quite abominable. For my own part, I would as lief they would put ratsbane in my mouth as the 'excellency' with which I am daily crammed. How much more true dignity was there in the simplicity of address amongst the Romans,—'Marcus Tullius Cicero,' 'Decimo Bruto Imperatori,' or 'Caio Marcello Consuli,'—than to 'his excellency Major-General Noodle,' or to 'the honorable John Doodle.' ... If, therefore, I should sometimes address a letter to you without the 'excellency' tacked, you must not esteem it a mark of personal or official disrespect, but the reverse."

Of all the words of congratulation which poured in upon the new governor, probably none came so straight from the heart, and none could have been quite so sweet to him, as those which, on the 12th of August, were uttered by some of the persecuted dissenters in Virginia, who, in many an hour of need, had learned to look up to Patrick Henry as their strong and splendid champion, in the legislature and in the courts. On the date just mentioned, "the ministers and delegates of the Baptist churches" of the State, being met in convention at Louisa, sent to him this address:—

May it please your Excellency,—As your advancement to the honorable and important station as governor of this commonwealth affords us unspeakable pleasure, we beg leave to present your excellency with our most cordial congratulations.

Your public virtues are such that we are under no temptation to flatter you. Virginia has done honor to her judgment in appointing your excellency to hold the reins of government at this truly critical conjuncture, as you have always distinguished yourself by your zeal and activity for her welfare, in whatever department has been assigned you. As a religious community, we have nothing to request of you. Your constant attachment to the glorious cause of liberty and the rights of conscience, leaves us no room to doubt of your excellency's favorable regards while we worthily demean ourselves. May God Almighty continue you long, very long, a public blessing to this your native country, and, after a life of usefulness here, crown you with immortal felicity in the world to come.

Signed by order:Jeremiah Walker, *Moderator*.John Williams, *Clerk*.

To these loving and jubilant words, the governor replied in an off-hand letter, the deep feeling of which is not the less evident because it is restrained,—a letter which is as choice and noble in diction as it is in thought:—

TO THE MINISTERS AND DELEGATES OF THE BAPTIST CHURCHES, AND THE MEMBERS OF THAT COMMUNION.

Gentlemen,—I am exceedingly obliged to you for your very kind address, and the favorable sentiments you are pleased to entertain respecting my conduct and the principles which have directed it. My constant endeavor shall be to guard the rights of all my fellow-citizens from every encroachment. I am happy to find a catholic spirit prevailing in our country, and that those religious distinctions, which formerly produced some heats, are now forgotten. Happy must every friend to virtue and America feel himself, to perceive that the only contest among us, at this most critical and important period, is, who shall be foremost to preserve our religious and civil liberties. My most earnest wish is, that Christian charity, forbearance, and love, may unite all our different persuasions, as brethren who must perish or triumph together; and I trust that the time is not far distant when we shall greet each other as the peaceable possessors of that just and equal system of liberty adopted by the last convention, and in support of which may God crown our arms with success.

I am, gentlemen, your most obedient and very humble servant,

P. Henry, Jun.

August 13, 1776.

On the day on which Governor Henry was sworn into office, the convention finally adjourned, having made provision for the meeting of the General Assembly on the first Monday of the following October. In the mean time, therefore, all the interests of the State were to be in the immediate keeping of the governor and privy council; and, for a part of that time, as it turned out, the governor himself was disabled for service. For we now encounter in the history of Patrick Henry, the first mention of that infirm health from which he seems to have suffered, in some degree, during the remaining twenty-three years of his life. Before taking full possession of the governor's palace, which had to be made ready for his use, he had likewise to prepare for this great change in his life by returning to his home in the county of Hanover. There he lay ill for some time; and upon his recovery he removed with his family to Williamsburg, which continued to be their home for the next three years.

The people of Virginia had been accustomed, for more than a century, to look upon their governors as personages of very great dignity. Several of those governors had been connected with the English peerage; all had served in Virginia in a vice-regal capacity; many had lived there in a sort of vice-regal pomp and magnificence. It is not to be supposed that Governor Henry would be able or willing to assume so much state and grandeur as his predecessors had done; and yet he felt, and the people of Virginia felt, that in the transition from royal to republican forms the dignity of that office should not be allowed to decline in any important particular. Moreover, as a contemporary observer mentions, Patrick Henry had been "accused by the big-wigs of former times as being a coarse and common man, and utterly destitute of dignity; and perhaps he wished to show them that they were mistaken." At any rate, by the testimony of all, he seems to have displayed his usual judgment and skill in adapting himself to the requirements of his position; and, while never losing his gentleness and his simplicity of manner, to have borne himself as the impersonation, for the time being, of the executive authority of a great and proud commonwealth. He ceased to appear frequently upon the streets; and whenever he did appear, he was carefully arrayed in a dressed wig, in black small-clothes, and in a scarlet cloak; and his presence and demeanor were such as to sustain, in the popular mind, the traditional respect for his high office.

He had so far recovered from the illness which had prostrated him during the summer, as to be at his post of duty when the General Assembly of the State began its first session, on Monday, the 7th of October, 1776. His health, however, was still extremely frail; for on the 30th of that month he was obliged to notify the House "that the low state of his health rendered him unable to attend to the duties of his office, and that his physicians had recommended to him to retire therefrom into the country, till he should recover his strength." His absence seems not to have been very long. By the 16th of November, as one may infer from entries in the journal of the House, he was able to resume his official duties.

The summer and autumn of that year proved to be a dismal period for the American cause. Before our eyes, as we now look back over those days, there marches this grim procession of dates: August 27, the battle of Long Island; August 29, Washington's retreat across East River; September 15, the panic among the American troops at Kip's Bay, and the American retreat from New York; September 16, the battle of Harlem Plains; September 20, the burning of New York; October 28, the battle of White Plains; November 16, the surrender of Fort Washington; November 20, the abandonment of Fort Lee, followed by Washington's retreat across the Jerseys. In the midst of these disasters, Washington found time to write, from the Heights of Harlem, on the 5th of October, to his old friend, Patrick Henry, congratulating him on his election as governor of Virginia and on his recovery from sickness; explaining the military situation at headquarters; advising him about military appointments in Virginia; and especially giving to him important suggestions concerning the immediate military defence of Virginia "against the enemy's ships and tenders, which," as Washington says to the governor, "may go up your rivers in quest of provisions, or for the purpose of destroying your towns." Indeed, Virginia was just then exposed to hostile attacks on all sides; and it was so plain that any attack by water would have found an easy approach to Williamsburg, that, in the course of the next few months, the public records and the public stores were removed to Richmond, as being, on every account, a "more secure site." Apparently, however, the prompt recognition of this danger by Governor Henry, early in the autumn of 1776, and his vigorous military preparations against it, were interpreted by some of his political enemies as a sign both of personal cowardice and of official self-glorification,—as is indicated by a letter written by the aged Landon Carter to General Washington, on the 31st of October, and filled with all manner of caustic garrulity and insinuation,—a letter from which it may be profitable for us to quote a few sentences, as qualifying somewhat that stream of honeyed testimony respecting Patrick Henry which commonly flows down upon us so copiously from all that period.

"If I don't err in conjecture," says Carter, "I can't help thinking that the head of our Commonwealth has as great a palace of fear and apprehension as can possess the heart of any being; and if we compare rumor with actual movements, I believe it will prove itself to every sensible man. As soon as the Congress sent for our first, third, fourth, fifth, and sixth regiments to assist you in contest against the enemy where they really were … there got a report among the soldiery that Dignity had declared it would not reside in Williamsburg without two thousand men under arms to guard him. This had like to have occasioned a mutiny. A desertion of many from the several companies did follow; boisterous fellows resisting, and swearing they would not leave their county…. What a finesse of popularity was this?… As soon as the regiments were gone, this great man found an interest with the council of state, perhaps timorous as himself, to issue orders for the militia of twenty-six counties, and five companies of a minute battalion, to march to Williamsburg, to protect him only against his own fears; and to make this the more popular, it was endeavored that the House of Delegates should give it a countenance, but, as good luck would have it, it was with difficulty refused. … Immediately then, … a bill is brought in to remove the seat of government,—some say, up to Hanover, to be called Henry-Town."

This gossip of a disappointed Virginian aristocrat, in vituperation of the public character of Governor Henry, naturally leads us forward in our story to that more stupendous eruption of gossip which relates, in the first instance, to the latter part of December, 1776, and which alleges that a conspiracy was then formed among certain members of the General Assembly to make Patrick Henry the dictator of Virginia. The first intimation ever given to the public concerning it, was given by Jefferson several years afterward, in his "Notes on Virginia," a fascinating brochure which was written by him in 1781 and 1782, was first printed privately in Paris in 1784, and was first published in England in 1787, in America in 1788. The essential portions of his statement are as follows:— "In December, 1776, our circumstances being much distressed, it was proposed in the House of Delegates to create a dictator, invested with every power legislative, executive, and judiciary, civil and military, of life and death, over our persons and over our properties…. One who entered into this contest from a pure love of liberty, and a sense of injured rights, who determined to make every sacrifice and to meet every danger, for the reëstablishment of those rights on a firm basis, … must stand confounded and dismayed when he is told that a considerable portion of" the House "had meditated the surrender of them into a single hand, and in lieu of a limited monarchy, to deliver him over to a despotic one…. The very thought alone was treason against the people; was treason against man in general; as riveting forever the chains which bow down their necks, by giving to their oppressors a proof, which they would have trumpeted through the universe, of the imbecility of republican government, in times of pressing danger, to shield them from harm…. Those who meant well, of the advocates of this measure (and most of them meant well, for I know them personally, had been their fellow-laborer in the common cause, and had often proved the purity of their principles), had been seduced in their judgment by the example of an ancient republic, whose constitution and circumstances were fundamentally different."

With that artistic tact and that excellent prudence which seem never to have failed Jefferson in any of his enterprises for the disparagement of his associates, he here avoids, as will be observed, all mention of the name of the person for whose fatal promotion this classic conspiracy was formed,—leaving that interesting item to come out, as it did many years afterward, when the most of those who could have borne testimony upon the subject were in their graves, and when the damning stigma could be comfortably fastened to the name of Patrick Henry without the direct intervention of Jefferson's own hands. Accordingly, in 1816, a French gentleman, Girardin, a near neighbor of Jefferson's, who enjoyed "the incalculable benefit of a free access to Mr. Jefferson's library," and who wrote the continuation of Burk's "History of Virginia" under Jefferson's very eye, gave in that work a highly wrought account of the alleged conspiracy of December, 1776, as involving "nothing less than the substitution of a despotic in lieu of a limited monarch;" and then proceeded to bring the accusation down from those lurid generalities of condemnation in which Jefferson himself had cautiously left it, by adding this sentence: "That Mr. Henry was the person in view for the dictatorship, is well ascertained."

Finally, in 1817, William Wirt, whose "Life of Henry" was likewise composed under nearly the same inestimable advantages as regards instruction and oversight furnished by Jefferson, repeated the fearful tale, and added some particulars; but, in doing so, Wirt could not fail—good lawyer and just man, as he was—to direct attention to the absence of all evidence of any collusion on the part of Patrick Henry with the projected folly and crime.

"Even the heroism of the Virginia legislature," says Wirt, "gave way; and, in a season of despair, the mad project of a dictator was seriously meditated. That Mr. Henry was thought of for this office, has been alleged, and is highly probable; but that the project was suggested by him, or even received his countenance, I have met with no one who will venture to affirm. There is a tradition that Colonel Archibald Cary, the speaker of the Senate, was principally instrumental in crushing this project; that meeting Colonel Syme, the step-brother of Colonel Henry, in the lobby of the House, he accosted him very fiercely in terms like these: 'I am told that your brother wishes to be dictator. Tell him from me, that the day of his appointment shall be the day of his death;—for he shall feel my dagger in his heart before the sunset of that day.' And the tradition adds that Colonel Syme, in great agitation, declared that 'if such a project existed, his brother had no hand in it; for that nothing could be more foreign to him, than to countenance any office which could endanger, in the most distant manner, the liberties of his country.' The intrepidity and violence of Colonel Cary's character renders the tradition probable; but it furnishes no proof of Mr. Henry's implication in the scheme."

A disinterested study of this subject, in the light of all the evidence now attainable, will be likely to convince any one that this enormous scandal must have been very largely a result of the extreme looseness at that time prevailing in the use of the word "dictator," and of its being employed, on the one side, in an innocent sense, and, on the other side, in a guilty one. In strict propriety, of course, the word designates a magistrate created in an emergency of public peril, and clothed for a time with unlimited power. It is an extreme remedy, and in itself a remedy extremely dangerous, and can never be innocently resorted to except when the necessity for it is indubitable; and it may well be questioned whether, among people and institutions like our own, a necessity can ever arise which would justify the temporary grant of unlimited power to any man. If this be true, it follows that no man among us can, without dire political guilt, ever consent to bestow such power; and that no man can, without the same guilt, ever consent to receive it.

Yet it is plain that even among us, between the years 1776 and 1783, emergencies of terrific public peril did arise, sufficient to justify, nay, even to compel, the bestowment either upon the governor of some State, or upon the general of the armies, not of unlimited power, certainly, but of extraordinary power,—such extraordinary power, for example, as was actually conferred by the Continental Congress, more than once, on Washington; as was conferred by the legislature of South Carolina on Governor John Rutledge; as was repeatedly conferred by the legislature of Virginia upon Governor Patrick Henry; and afterward, in still higher degree, by the same legislature, on Governor Thomas Jefferson himself. Nevertheless, so loose was the meaning then attached to the word "dictator," that it was not uncommon for men to speak of these very cases as examples of the bestowment of a dictatorship, and of the exercise of dictatorial power; although, in every one of the cases mentioned, there was lacking the essential feature of a true dictatorship, namely, the grant of unlimited power to one man. It is perfectly obvious, likewise, that when, in those days, men spoke thus of a dictatorship, and of dictatorial power, they attached no suggestion of political guilt either to the persons who bestowed such power, or to the persons who severally accepted it,—the tacit understanding being that, in every instance, the public danger required and justified some grant of extraordinary power; that no more power was granted than was necessary; and that the man to whom, in any case, the grant was made, was a man to whom, there was good reason to believe, the grant could be made with safety. Obviously, it was upon this tacit understanding of its meaning that the word was used, for instance, by Edmund Randolph, in 1788, in the Virginia Constitutional Convention, when, alluding to the extraordinary power bestowed by Congress on Washington, he said: "We had an American dictator in 1781." Surely, Randolph did not mean to impute political crime, either to the Congress which made Washington a dictator, or to Washington himself who consented to be made one. It was upon the same tacit understanding, also, that Patrick Henry, in reply to Randolph, took up the word, and extolled the grant of dictatorial power to Washington on the occasion referred to: "In making a dictator," said Henry, "we followed the example of the most glorious, magnanimous, and skilful nations. In great dangers, this power has been given. Rome has furnished us with an illustrious example. America found a person for that trust: she looked to Virginia for him. We gave a dictatorial power to hands that used it gloriously, and which were rendered more glorious by surrendering it up."

Thus it is apparent that the word "dictator" was frequently used in those times in a sense perfectly innocent. As all men know, however, the word is one capable of suggesting the possibilities of dreadful political crime; and it is not hard to see how, when employed by one person to describe the bestowment and acceptance of extraordinary power,—implying a perfectly innocent proposition, it could be easily taken by another person as describing the bestowment and acceptance of unlimited power,—implying a proposition which among us, probably, would always be a criminal one. With the help which this discussion may give us, let us now return to the General Assembly of Virginia, at Williamsburg, approaching the close of its first session, in the latter part of December, 1776. It was on the point of adjourning, not to meet again until the latter part of March, 1777. At that moment, by the arrival of most alarming news from the seat of war, it was forced to make special provision for the public safety during the interval which must elapse before its next session. Its journal indicates that, prior to the 20th of December, it had been proceeding with its business in a quiet way, under no apparent consciousness of imminent peril. On that day, however, there are traces of a panic; for, on that day, "The Virginia Gazette" announced to them the appalling news of "the crossing of the Delaware by the British forces, from twelve to fifteen thousand strong; the position of General Washington, at Bristol, on the south side of the river, with only six thousand men;" and the virtual flight of Congress from Philadelphia. At this rate, how long would it be before the Continental army would be dispersed or captured, and the troops of the enemy sweeping in vengeance across the borders of Virginia? Accordingly, the House of Delegates immediately resolved itself into "a committee to take into their consideration the state of America;" but not being able to reach any decision that day, it voted to resume the subject on the day following, and for that purpose to meet an hour earlier than usual. So, on Saturday, the 21st of December, the House passed a series of resolutions intended to provide for the crisis into which the country was plunged, and, among the other resolutions, this:—

"And whereas the present imminent danger of America, and the ruin and misery which threatens the good people of this Commonwealth, and their posterity, calls for the utmost exertion of our strength, and it is become necessary for the preservation of the State that the usual forms of government be suspended during a limited time, for the more speedy execution of the most vigorous and effectual measures to repel the invasion of the enemy;

"*Resolved, therefore*, That the governor be, and he is hereby fully authorized and empowered, by and with the advice and consent of the privy council, from henceforward, until ten days next after the first meeting of the General Assembly, to carry into execution such requisitions as may be made to this Commonwealth by the American Congress for the purpose of encountering or repelling the enemy; to order the three battalions on the pay of this Commonwealth to march, if necessary, to join the Continental army, or to the assistance of any of our sister States; to call forth any and such greater military force as they shall judge requisite, either by embodying and arraying companies or regiments of volunteers, or by raising additional battalions, appointing and commissioning the proper officers, and to direct their operations within this Commonwealth, under the command of the Continental generals or other officers according to their respective ranks, or order them to march to join and act in concert with the Continental army, or the troops of any of the American States; and to provide for their pay, supply of provisions, arms, and other necessaries, at the charge of this Commonwealth, by drawing on the treasurer for the money which may be necessary from time to time; and the said treasurer is authorized to pay such warrants out of any public money which may be in his hands, and the General Assembly will, at their next session, make ample provision for any deficiency which may happen. But that this departure from the constitution of government, being in this instance founded only on the most evident and urgent necessity, ought not hereafter to be drawn into precedent."

These resolutions, having been pressed rapidly through the forms of the House, were at once carried up to the Senate for its concurrence. The answer of the Senate was promptly returned, agreeing to all the resolutions of the lower House, but proposing an important amendment in the phraseology of the particular resolution which we have just quoted. Instead of this clause—"the usual forms of government should be suspended," it suggested the far more accurate and far more prudent expression which here follows,—"additional powers be given to the governor and council." This amendment was assented to by the House; and almost immediately thereafter it adjourned until the last Thursday in March, 1777, "then to meet in the city of Williamsburg, or at such other place as the governor and council, for good reasons, may appoint."

Such, undoubtedly, was the occasion on which, if at any time during that session, the project for a dictatorship in Virginia was under consideration by the House of Delegates. The only evidence for the reality of such a project is derived from the testimony of Jefferson; and Jefferson, though a member of the House, was not then in attendance, having procured, on the 29th of the previous month, permission to be absent during the remainder of the session. Is it not probable that the whole terrible plot, as it afterward lay in the mind of Jefferson, may have originated in reports which reached him elsewhere, to the effect that, in the excitement of the House over the public danger and over the need of energetic measures against that danger, some members had demanded that the governor should be invested with what they perhaps called dictatorial power, meaning thereby no more than extraordinary power; and that all the criminal accretions to that meaning, which Jefferson attributed to the project, were simply the work of his own imagination, always sensitive and quick to take alarm on behalf of human liberty, and, on such a subject as this, easily set on fire by examples of awful political crime which would occur to him from Roman history? This suggestion, moreover, is not out of harmony with one which has been made by a thorough and most candid student of the subject, who says: "I am very much inclined to think that some sneering remark of Colonel Cary, on that occasion, has given rise to the whole story about a proposed dictator at that time."

At any rate, this must not be forgotten: if the project of a dictatorship, in the execrable sense affirmed by Jefferson, was, during that session, advocated by any man or by any cabal in the

Assembly, history must absolve Patrick Henry of all knowledge of it, and of all responsibility for it. Not only has no tittle of evidence been produced, involving his connivance at such a scheme, but the Assembly itself, a few months later, unwittingly furnished to posterity the most conclusive proof that no man in that body could have believed him to be smirched with even the suggestion of so horrid a crime. Had Patrick Henry been suspected, during the autumn and early winter of 1776, of any participation in the foul plot to create a despotism in Virginia, is it to be conceived that, at its very next session, in the spring of 1777, that Assembly, composed of nearly the same members as before, would have reëlected to the governorship so profligate and dangerous a man, and that too without any visible opposition in either House? Yet that is precisely what the Virginia Assembly did in May, 1777. Moreover, one year later, this same Assembly reëlected this same profligate and dangerous politician for his third and last permissible year in the governorship, and it did so with the same unbroken unanimity. Moreover, during all that time, Thomas Jefferson was a member, and a most conspicuous and influential member, of the Virginia Assembly. If, indeed, he then believed that his old friend, Patrick Henry, had stood ready in 1776, to commit "treason against the people" of America, and "treason against mankind in general," why did he permit the traitor to be twice reëlected to the chief magistracy, without the record of even one brave effort against him on either occasion?

On the 26th of December, 1776, in accordance with the special authority thus conferred upon him by the General Assembly, Governor Henry issued a vigorous proclamation, declaring that the "critical situation of American affairs" called for "the utmost exertion of every sister State to put a speedy end to the cruel ravages of a haughty and inveterate enemy, and secure our invaluable rights," and "earnestly exhorting and requiring" all the good people of Virginia to assist in the formation of volunteer companies for such service as might be required. The date of that proclamation was also the date of Washington's famous matutinal surprise of the Hessians at Trenton,—a bit of much-needed good luck, which was followed by his fortunate engagement with the enemy near Princeton, on the 3d of January, 1777. On these and a very few other extremely small crumbs of comfort, the struggling revolutionists had to nourish their burdened hearts for many a month thereafter; Washington himself, during all that time, with his little army of tattered and barefoot warriors, majestically predominating over the scene from the heights of Morristown; while the good-humored British commander, Sir William Howe, considerately abstained from any serious military disturbance until the middle of the following summer. Thus the chief duty of the governor of Virginia, during the winter and spring of 1777, as it had been in the previous autumn, was that of trying to keep in the field Virginia's quota of troops, and of trying to furnish Virginia's share of military supplies,—no easy task, it should seem, in those times of poverty, confusion, and patriotic languor. The official correspondence of the governor indicates the unslumbering anxiety, the energy, the fertility of device with which, in spite of defective health, he devoted himself to these hard tasks.

In his great desire for exact information as to the real situation at headquarters, Governor Henry had sent to Washington a secret messenger by the name of Walker, who was to make his observations at Morristown and to report the results to himself. Washington at once perceived the embarrassments to which such a plan might lead; and accordingly, on the 24th of February, 1777, he wrote to the governor, gently explaining why he could not receive Mr. Walker as a mere visiting observer:—

"To avoid the precedent, therefore, and from your character of Mr. Walker, and the high opinion I myself entertain of his abilities, honor, and prudence, I have taken him into my family as an extra aide-de-camp, and shall be happy if, in this character, he can answer your expectations. I sincerely thank you, sir, for your kind congratulations on the late success of the Continental arms (would to God it may continue), and for your polite mention of me. Let me earnestly entreat that the troops raised in Virginia for this army be forwarded on by companies, or otherwise, without delay, and as well equipped as possible for the field, or we shall be in no condition to open the campaign." On the 29th of the following month, the governor wrote to Washington of the overwhelming difficulty attending all his efforts to comply with the request mentioned in the letter just cited: —

"I am very sorry to inform you that the recruiting business of late goes on so badly, that there remains but little prospect of filling the six new battalions from this State, voted by the Assembly. The Board of Council see this with great concern, and, after much reflection on the subject, are of opinion that the deficiency in our regulars can no way be supplied so properly as by enlisting volunteers. There is reason to believe a considerable number of these may be got to serve six or eight months.... I believe you can receive no assistance by drafts from the militia. From the battalions of the Commonwealth none can be drawn as yet, because they are not half full.... Virginia will find some apology with you for this deficiency in her quota of regulars, when the difficulties lately thrown in our way are considered. The Georgians and Carolinians have enlisted [in Virginia] probably two battalions at least. A regiment of artillery is in great forwardness. Besides these, Colonels Baylor and Grayson are collecting regiments; and three others are forming for this State. Add to all this our Indian wars and marine service, almost total want of necessaries, the false accounts of deserters, — many of whom lurk here, — the terrors of the smallpox and the many deaths occasioned by it, and the deficient enlistments are accounted for in the best manner I can. As no time can be spared, I wish to be honored with your answer as soon as possible, in order to promote the volunteer scheme, if it meets your approbation. I should be glad of any improvements on it that may occur to you. I believe about four of the six battalions may be enlisted, but have seen no regular [return] of their state. Their scattered situation, and being many of them in broken quotas, is a reason for their slow movement. I have issued repeated orders for their march long since."

The General Assembly of Virginia, at its session in the spring of 1777, was required to elect a governor, to serve for one year from the day on which that session should end. As no candidate was named in opposition to Patrick Henry, the Senate proposed to the House of Delegates that he should be reappointed without ballot. This, accordingly, was done, by resolution of the latter body on the 29th of May, and by that of the Senate on the 1st of June. On the 5th of June, the committee appointed to inform the governor of this action laid before the House his answer: —

Gentlemen, — The signal honor conferred on me by the General Assembly, in their choice of me to be governor of this Commonwealth, demands my best acknowledgments, which I beg the favor of you to convey to them in the most acceptable manner.

I shall execute the duties of that high station to which I am again called by the favor of my fellow-citizens, according to the best of my abilities, and I shall rely upon the candor and wisdom of the Assembly to excuse and supply my defects. The good of the Commonwealth shall be the only object of my pursuit, and I shall measure my happiness according to the success which shall attend my endeavors to establish the public liberty. I beg to be presented to the Assembly, and that they and you will be assured that I am, with every sentiment of the highest regard, their and your most obedient and very humble servant, P. Henry.

After a perusal of this nobly written letter, the gentle reader will have no difficulty in concluding that, if indeed the author of it was then lying in wait for an opportunity to set up a despotism in Virginia, he had already become an adept in the hypocrisy which enabled him, not only to conceal the fact, but to convey an impression quite the opposite.

www.ingramcontent.com/pod-product-compliance
Lightning Source LLC
LaVergne TN
LVHW072107070426
835509LV00002B/52